Leadership
What's in it for schools?

Thomas J. Sergiovanni

RoutledgeFalmer
Taylor & Francis Group

LONDON AND NEW YORK

First published 2001
by RoutledgeFalmer
2 Park Square, Milton Park, Abingdon, Oxon OX14 4RN

Simultaneously published in the USA and Canada
by RoutledgeFalmer
270 Madison Avenue, New York, NY 10016

RoutledgeFalmer is an imprint of the Taylor & Francis Group

© 2001 Thomas J. Sergiovanni

Typeset in Baskerville by
M Rules

British Library Cataloguing in Publication Data
A catalogue record for this book is available from the British
Library

Library of Congress Cataloging in Publication Data
A catalog record has been applied for

ISBN 0-415-23070-5 (hbk)
ISBN 0-415-23071-3 (pbk)

Lea

Effective leadership is integral to school improvement. Thomas J. Sergiovanni looks at the central issues entailed in school leadership and in doing so identifies ten key responsibilities for headteachers. He explores the part played by authentic, character-rich leadership in building a school which is academically successful and morally responsive, but also an environment of which teachers, pupils and parents are happy to be a part. This is an authoritative, practical and insightful look at the role and responsibilities of the headteacher, written by one of the most eminent and experienced authors on the subject.

Thomas J. Sergiovanni is Lillian Radford Professor of Education and Administration and Senior Fellow at the Center for Educational Leadership, Trinity University, San Antonio. As well as serving on the editorial boards of several major education journals, he is an experienced and prolific author on school leadership. His most recent books include *Leadership for the Schoolhouse: How is it Different? Why is it Important?* (1996). *The Lifeworld of Leadership: Creating Culture, Community and Personal Meaning in Our Schools* (2000) and *The Principalship: A Reflective Practice Perspective* (2000).

What's in it for schools?
Edited by Kate Myers and John MacBeath

Inspection: What's in it for schools?
James Learmonth

Leadership: What's in it for schools?
Thomas J. Sergiovanni

Contents

List of figures and tables   vi
Series Editors' preface   vii
Preface   ix

1   The real context for leadership   1
2   Leading with ideas   20
3   New leadership, roles, and competencies   38
4   Leading communities of responsibility   59
5   School character, school effectiveness, and layered
    standards   76
6   Leadership and learning: searching for a practical theory   99
7   Leadership in the real world: a postscript by Richard
    Middleton   126

Notes   134
References   136
Index   143

Figures and tables

Figure 3.1   How central strategies influence local leadership   50
Table 6.1   Making schools smarter by increasing organizational
             intelligence   113

Series Editors' preface

Kate Myers and John MacBeath

Series introduction

There is a concerted move to raise standards in the public education system. The aim is laudable. Few people would disagree with it. However, there is no clear agreement about what we mean by 'standards'. Do we mean attainment or achievement more broadly defined, for example, and how we are to raise whatever it is we agree needs raising?

At the same time, there appears to be an increasing trend towards approaching changes in education through a controlling, rational and technical framework. This framework tends to concentrate on educational content and delivery and ignores the human resource perspective and the complexity of how human beings live, work and interact with one another. It overemphasizes linearity and pays insufficient attention to how people respond to change and either support or subvert it.

Recent government initiatives, including the National Curriculum, OfSTED school and LEA inspections, assessment procedures, league tables, target-setting, literacy and numeracy hours, and performance management have endorsed this framework. On occasions this has been less to do with the content of 'reforms' than the process of implementation – that is, doing it 'to' rather than 'with' the teaching profession. Teachers are frequently treated as the problem rather than part of the solution, with the consequence that many feel disillusioned, demoralised and disempowered. Critics of this *top-down* approach are often seen as lacking rigour, complacent about standards, and uninterested in raising achievement.

We wanted to edit this series because we believe that you can be passionate about public education, about raising achievement, about ensuring that all pupils are entitled to the best possible education that society is able to provide – whatever their race, sex or class. We also believe that achieving this is not a simple matter of common sense or of the appliance of science – it is more complex than that. Most of all, we see the teaching profession as an important part of the solution to finding ways through these complexities.

What's in it for schools? is a series that will make educational policy issues relevant to practitioners. Each book in the series focuses on a major educational issue and raises key questions, such as:

- can inspection be beneficial to schools?
- how can assessment procedures help pupils learn?
- how can school self-evaluation improve teaching and learning?
- what impact does leadership in the school have in the classroom?
- how can school improvement become classroom improvement?

The books are grounded in sound theory, recent research evidence and best practice, and aim to:

- help you to make meaning personally and professionally from knowledge in a given field;
- help you to seek out practical applications of an area of knowledge for classrooms and schools;
- help those of you who want to research the field in greater depth, by providing key sources with accessible summaries and recommendations.

In addition, each chapter ends with a series of questions for reflection or further discussion, enabling schools to use the books as a resource for whole-school staff development.

We hope that the books in this series will show you that there are ways of raising achievement that can take account of how schools grow and develop and how teachers work and interact with one another. *What's in it for schools?* – a great deal, we think!

Preface

Leadership, what's in it for schools? This is a simple question without easy answers. One response is to sing the praises of leadership. Leadership counts. Rare is the effective school that does not have an effective head. Adding teacher leadership to the equation ensures that school improvement becomes a way of life in the school. These praises are well deserved. Still, we do not have a very good picture of what it is that makes school leadership successful.

But, you might be thinking, the literature is filled with lists of things that one is supposed to do to be an effective leader. Indeed, we have lots of lists. The problem is, as Barth (1990) explains, the same things applied to different contexts and to different situations typically produce different results. Further, many of the things we believe are important to successful leadership may not be as important as we think. And, there are some things that successful leaders do that are missed or are not appreciated.

Perhaps most perplexing is the understanding of leadership that emerges from the belief that every problem has a solution. This is a belief prominent in the cultures of many Western societies. The US and UK are good examples. Leadership is identified with solving problems and the purpose of leadership is finding solutions. A better understanding, I argue in this book, is that leadership is about helping people to understand the problems they face, with helping people to get a handle on how to manage these problems, and even with learning how to live with problems. Leadership is, after all, a struggle – a quest to do the right thing. We can appreciate this struggle when we realize that leaders are ordinary people who are required to make uncommon commitments to try to fulfill their obligations. They do this by serving purposes and by seeking to help others to be successful. They do this by helping people to reach an acceptable accommodation with an imperfect world. They do this by inviting and receiving the help of those for whom they are responsible. To appreciate leadership in this context is to appreciate just how important are both humility and hope – a theme highlighted throughout this book.

Suggesting that leadership in today's world of schooling requires an uncommon commitment can be scary. Thankfully successful heads don't view themselves as being the center of the universe. An uncommon commitment requires that leadership be everywhere and that leaders master the new basics of leadership: managing complexity, leading with ideas, and developing what social scientists call *social capital*. For leadership to be everywhere it must be embedded deeply both throughout the school and in the school community. In successful schools leadership density rules.

Overview of the book

This book is short and to the point. Today's leadership theories are too rational and too scripted to fit the messy world in which schooling actually takes place. These theories sound great, but do not work well in the real world of practice. Dealing with the complexities of this world requires that teachers and administrators practice a leadership based less and less on their personalities, less and less on their positions, less and less on mandates, and more and more on ideas. Leadership that counts is far more cognitive in orientation than it is personality based or rules based. Cognitive leadership has more to do with purposes, values, and frameworks that obligate us morally than it does with needs that touch us psychologically or with bureaucratic things that push us organizationally.

To be successful in responding to the complexities of the real world, new leadership roles and new leadership competencies must be developed and mastered. Key will be helping schools become communities of responsibility. Studies of successful learning communities reveal that a school's "organizational character" may well be the most important ingredient in any school success formula. Building character within the school while meeting expectations from the state and other external sources requires a broad-based commitment to the development of layered standards and layered accountability systems. A complement to cultivating and using organizational character to improve schools is enhancing a school's ability to link leadership with learning. When the two are brought together as one and when organizational character becomes the foundation for a school's practice, we have the makings of a practical theory of leadership that fits the realities of the schoolhouse.

Chapter 1 examines the context for leadership that teachers and heads actually face. Despite the complexities and demands of leadership, some leaders are more effective than others. The reason, I argue, is that successful leaders pay attention to seven principles that help them navigate through the inner structure of schools where real change takes place. I show how successful leaders think and behave when tending to each of the principles.

Chapter 2 examines the sources of authority that leaders may use as the basis for their leadership practice. I argue that it is idea-based leadership that has the greatest potential for helping us realize our goals. Key is purposing and the building of idea structures that bring people together in a common cause and as part of a moral web of mutual responsibilities. Ideas, I show, are at the heart of a school's culture and the foundation for building a learning community.

Chapter 3 examines the relationship between leadership and change, arguing that too much emphasis is given to the change process itself and not enough to the substance of change. Leaders will have to master seven basic competencies in order to lead effectively in the future: the management of attention, the management of meaning, the management of trust, the management of self, as well as the management of paradox, the management of effectiveness, and the management of commitment. Chapter 3 concludes with some tips for implementing the competencies in practice.

Chapter 4 explores schools as communities of responsibility and examines how such schools are led. Once established, communities of responsibility become powerful substitutes for bureaucratic and personality-based leadership. Building community in schools is important, I argue, for practical reasons. Community satisfies the needs that teachers and students have to be connected to each other and to the school, helps everyone focus on the common good, provides students with a safe harbor in a stormy sea, builds relationships, enhances responsibility, and supports learning.

Chapter 5 examines the concept of school character, how it works, and how it is related to school effectiveness. Schools with character, I note, know who they are, have developed a common understanding of their purposes, and have faith in their ability to celebrate this uniqueness as a powerful way to achieve their goals.

In Chapter 6, I argue that a new theory of leadership rooted in learning and rooted in moral commitments needs to be developed if we are to be responsive to today's complex world of schooling. This theory would be oriented more to controlling probabilities than controlling events, would rely on mutual adaptation among people engaged in the actual work of schooling, would seek to expand both opportunity and capacity for everyone to learn, and would rely on the development of organizational intelligence as a means to help schools become smarter and more effective at what they do. I then outline some principles for organizing in this learning environment and summarize with a discussion of leadership and its challenges as we look ahead.

Chapter 7, "Leadership in the real world," is a postscript to the book written by Dr. Richard Middleton. Dr. Middleton is superintendent of schools for the Northeast Independent School District in the greater San Antonio, Texas, area. He is responsible for 63 schools with an enrollment of approximately 50,000 students. A former school head, Dr. Middleton is also a clinical professor of educational administration at Trinity University. Middleton draws on his experiences as a school administrator in commenting on the nature and practice of school leadership.

Looking ahead

In describing two successful heads, Sophia Sa of the Panasonic Foundation notes:

> Looking at their schools, one is struck by many things, but in particular by the extent to which so many others in the schools are empowered to take responsibility for so much of importance. . . . [The heads] haven't abdicated leadership. Rather, what they clearly understand is that leadership, like so many other things of value, is not a zero-sum commodity to be hoarded by one or a few, but one that grows through sharing.
>
> (2000: 1)

Leadership, it appears, is still another form of capital. And, like social capital, it increases in value as it is shared in the school. This book believes in leadership, but not leadership, invested only in individuals or only in hierarchies. Leadership that will win for all of our children is based on ideas and is expressed as a function for which all are responsible. Every leadership act leads to more leadership helping the school to become a community of leaders.

I am grateful for Dr. Middleton's help with this project. Together we want to thank our students at Trinity University, our colleagues in the Center for Educational Leadership, and the many school leaders with whom we work to improve schools for all of our students.

Thomas J. Sergiovanni
January 2001
San Antonio, Texas

1 The real context for leadership

"The patch should fit the hole" noted Thomas Jefferson. The hole represents the problems leaders face as they seek to improve schools and the patch represents the theories and practices leaders use to solve these problems. Do we have the right patch? And if we don't, what kind of patch do we need? I believe that the leadership theories and practices now used are too rational and too scripted for the messy world in which school leaders must work. In this chapter I describe the problem and propose some alternatives by talking frankly with heads and teachers about the real-world dilemmas that they face as they attempt to lead.

School leadership, to paraphrase Hugo Sonnenschein the former president of the University of Chicago, is not for people who want to work on real-world problems that have simple solutions. If this is what a person wants, she or he should try astrology (cited in Schlosberg 1993: 37). But the job can be fun if one is at ease with complexity, likes challenges, and is willing to work hard. Still, we have to be realistic. Providing leadership for continuous school improvement is hard enough when that is the only task to worry about. But leaders also have to keep schools working well day by day. This combination of moving forward while maintaining stability can make the job at times seem daunting.

Part of the problem is that the world of schooling is just too complex, disconnected, and even chaotic for direct leadership to work. Too often what leaders do is not tightly connected to anything important. Further, in this age of top-down school reform, the number of constraints that administrators and teachers and their schools face from distant authorities is increasing. Constraints can rob leaders and schools of discretion. And without discretion it becomes difficult and often impossible to lead.

Leadership becomes more and more like trying to run in soft sand. Yet, things need to be done in schools. Problems need to be solved and improvements need to be invented and implemented. Some leaders just can't cope with this kind of complexity and are not succeeding. Thankfully, however, most school leaders have figured out ways to succeed.

It is not by chance that some leaders are more effective than others, even when all are faced with similar demands and constraints. Effective leaders have a better understanding of how the worlds of schooling and of school leadership work. They have figured out alternatives to direct leadership that are able to get people connected to each other, to their work, and to their responsibilities. They are less likely to base their practice on the assumption that predetermined solutions exist for most of the problems they face. They accept with ease Roland Barth's admonition that the issues and problems of education are remarkably similar across the educational landscape, but that "it is the solutions, if there are solutions, that tend to be idiosyncratic and particularistic, and much less generalizable from context to context" (Barth 1980: xv). Thus, they have resigned themselves to the difficult task of having to create their practice in use as they make decisions. The decisions may not warrant a write-up in a textbook on administration, but they are honest ones that, however imperfect, fit the context and situations they face and serve the school and its local community well. Yielding to practicality, these effective leaders realize the most important problems are beyond the reach of the easy answers often embedded in the technical and rational solutions offered by distant central authorities or embedded in the rhetoric of simplistically conceived school reform.

How do you satisfy pressures to comply with distant requirements when you know that rarely is there a one-best way? Donald Schön frames the situation this way: "The practitioner must choose. Shall he remain on the high ground where he can solve relatively unimportant problems according to prevailing standards of rigor, or shall he descend to the swamp of important problems and nonrigorous inquiry?" (Schön 1987: 3). Successful leaders are not afraid to choose the latter alternative and have learned how to get away with it. Throughout the educational system the standard prescription for making decisions has looked like this:

LEADERSHIP – THE STANDARD PRESCRIPTION

- Know clearly what your problem is and know specifically what your goals are.
- Explore every possible solution to the problem or every possible route to achieve the goals.
- Evaluate the costs and benefits of each alternative.
- Systematically compare the alternatives.
- Choose the single most effective course of action.
- Apply this course of action throughout the system as a one-best way.

Once a decision is made and a course of action is selected, leaders are expected to pursue it relentlessly using all available resources to get the job done. Consistency is thought to be a virtue. Leaders, responding to pressures to be "strong," are expected to stay on target at all costs and to not give up. But in the real world of school practice leaders cannot be either this rational or this aggressive. As Etzioni points out:

> The executives of today and tomorrow face continuing information overloads but little growth in the amount of knowledge usable for most complex managerial decisions. Decision makers in the 1990s will continue to travel on unmarked, unlit roads in rain and fog rather than on the broad, familiar, sunlit streets of their own hometowns.
>
> (1989: 123)

In commenting on complexity in the business world John Byrne points out: "In the 20th century, succeeding was like climbing the Rocky Mountains. It wasn't easy, but the path was obvious. Success was a matter of executing a well-established business plan: Every step up brought you closer to the top" (1999: 90). But now, he argues, it turns out that the Rocky Mountains are constantly shifting. One moment you are on top and the next moment you are in a valley. It is pretty hard to figure out beforehand where you will wind up.

Some intellectual qualities

Navigating the Rocky Mountains calls for dipping deep into one's intellectual reservoir to find the right qualities for thinking anew about our work. Three qualities stand out: the capacity to synthesize, to innovate, and to be perceptive (*United News-Journal* 1991: 2). Leaders who have mastered the capacity to synthesize are able to sort through and make sense of large amounts of information, identifying what is important and putting this knowledge together to reach powerful, often new, conclusions. Leaders who have mastered the capacity to innovate are able to combine the elements that are now known in new ways to solve problems. Leaders who have mastered the capacity to be perceptive have an intuitive knack for identifying what is really important, for understanding what makes a situation run or work in a certain way, and for figuring out what to do about it. These intellectual qualities can lead to new understandings of how the world of schooling works and how to function successfully as a leader in that world. You will need these qualities to engage in the ideas proposed below. They describe an amoeba theory of leadership and life that can help you figure out how to lead your school to higher levels of performance and satisfaction without compromising the sense and meaning that can only come from empowered local sources.

One lesson learned by successful leaders is that the best approach to school improvement is to be conservative. This does not mean abandoning efforts to improve the quality of life offered by schools to teachers and students, the curriculum, or existing patterns of planning, teaching, and evaluating. It does mean, however, that emphasizing drastic restructuring of present organizational patterns as the means to bring about significant improvements is usually neither practical nor necessary.

Managing organizational patterns and structures for schooling is important, as we shall discuss in Chapter 6. But managing and restructuring are not the same. More important than the structure of the school itself is the underlying theory of management and life, and the values, beliefs, and norms that constitute this theory. How a school looks represents its outer structure. The values and beliefs that constitute a school's governing theory constitute its inner structure. Changes in the former but not the latter reinforce the well-known adage: "The more things change, the more they stay the same." Although ideally inner and outer structure should change together, inner structure changes do not depend entirely on outer structure changes.

Getting at the inner structure of schools requires paying attention to seven basic principles:[1]

SEVEN BASIC PRINCIPLES

1   Invert the rule.
2   Know the difference between causes and consequences.
3   Think amoeba.
4   Emphasize sense and meaning.
5   Build with canvas.
6   Be humble in decision-making.
7   Remember moral aspects of leadership.

---

1. Invert the rule

Standard theories of management, leadership, and change assume that schools and other enterprises are managerially tight and culturally loose. They portray the operation of schools as resembling the mechanical workings of a clock composed of cogs and gears, wheels, drives, and pins, all tightly connected in an orderly and predictable manner. It follows from this tidy and orderly clockworks view that the task of leadership is to gain control and regulate the master wheel and master pin.

Sometimes the master wheel and pin take the form of a new curriculum, mandated standards linked to a sophisticated testing program, a design for monitoring what teachers do and for evaluating their teaching behaviors, a program that trains teachers to implement a specific teaching model, or a new grouping pattern that requires teachers to teach differently. It is assumed that if one gains control of the master wheel and pin, all the other wheels and pins will move responsively and the leader's intents will be accomplished. Teachers, for example, will teach the way they are supposed to and students will be taught what they are supposed to learn. Unfortunately, as the classic Hawthorne studies (see, for example, Roethlisberger and Dickson 1939) and dozens of others since have clearly demonstrated, this rarely happens – at least not on a sustained and continuous basis, and not without excessive monitoring and regressive enforcement efforts.

Successful improvements in schools require that we invert this rule. Schools are not managerially tight and culturally loose, but rather are culturally tight and managerially loose. The reality is that teachers and other school workers respond much more to their values and beliefs, how they are socialized, and the norms of the work group than they do to management controls.

It is not likely that organizational designs and structures proposed for the school that ignore the inverted rule will be accepted with enthusiasm. And it is not likely that designs and structures now in place or forced into place that ignore the inverted rule will be implemented as intended. If changes do not affect the teaching and learning that takes place when no one is watching, they can hardly be considered changes. Inverting the rule places emphasis on the school's culture. Cultural "cement" in the form of shared purposes, values, and commitments and the norms they create is needed to tie things together so that all the parts will work in harmony.

2. Causes and consequences

Schools all over the world are under pressure to restructure organizationally as a way to improve. Much of what is proposed promises to serve students and teachers well, but much doesn't. Here is a litmus test for deciding when a restructuring proposal should be considered and when a restructuring proposal should be rejected. Is the restructuring proposal *first* a cause or a consequence? If changes are proposed in how we organize people, schedules, and space, in how we structure things, and in how we make decisions as a means to restructure, cast them away. These changes are not likely to affect anything important for very long and if they do, the effects are likely to be negative. If, however, we make these restructuring decisions as a natural consequence of our efforts to create better learning environments for teachers and students, then we increase the odds of being successful.

Restructuring needs to be a natural consequence of our actual efforts to improve teaching and learning. Breaking schools up into academies, houses, teams, families, or other smaller units is a case in point. Too often reformers push this idea as an end in itself rather than as a solution to problems. If we want to know students well, then we should consider ways to get small. If we want students more involved in schools, then we should consider ways to get small. If we want to increase the level of civility in schools, then we should consider ways to get small. If we want to build strong academic norms in the school, then we should consider ways to get small. Getting small should be a natural consequence of our wanting to know students well, increase their involvement in the life of the school, raise levels of civility, and build strong academic norms. If getting small is not feasible for political, physical, or other reasons, we can still keep our eye on the prize by considering other ways to achieve our goals.

3. *Think amoeba*

The first requirement for a rational theory of administrative practice is that it be practical and realistic by fitting the way the world of schooling works. If a theory sounds logical and makes excellent copy for books and articles but doesn't fit, then it is not rational but rationalistic.

Cast in this light, thinking amoeba is a rational approach to understanding the nature of administrative work. Running a school is like trying to get a giant amoeba to move from one side of the street to another. As the "glob" slips off the curb onto the street and begins its meandering journey, the job of the leader is to figure out how to keep it together, while trying to move it in the general direction of the other side. This involves pulling here, pushing there, patching holes, supporting thin parts, and breaking up logjams.

The pace is fast and furious as the leader moves first here, then there. Throughout, she or he is never quite sure where the glob will wind up, but never loses sight of the overall goal of getting it to the other side. Mind, heart, and hand become one as the leader "plays" the glob, relying on her or his nose for globbiness, and ability to discern and anticipate patterns of movement that emerge.

How different is this view from the one offered in the literature and the one assumed by policy makers – a view that would have us attempt the crossing of the street by first specifying our destination as a highly specific outcome and then implementing an explicit, linear, and managerial chain of planning, organizing, directing, controlling, and evaluating as if contexts were fixed and people were inanimate. This simplistic pattern might be rational for running a railroad but is rationalistic when applied to running a school. Solid management thinking works only when we place the work of school leaders within a cultural context. It is norms that drive the system and solid management reflects this reality. Whatever our aspirations and plans for school improvement, they must be responsive to the amoeba-like characteristics of schools. "Think amoeba" might not be tidy advice, but it is practical advice.

4. Emphasize sense and meaning

One might reasonably ask, "But are not ideas like 'think amoeba' and 'managerially loose, culturally tight' nonleadership views of school improvement?" They are indeed nonorganizational views of school improvement, but they are not nonleadership views. If what matters most to teachers and students, parents and other locals are values and beliefs, patterns of socialization, and norms that emerge in the school, then these are the characteristics that must be considered as key to school improvement efforts. These characteristics fall within the domain of leadership. As leadership is practiced in an amoeba-like and structurally loose world, some things matter more than others.

For example, whether leaders are warm or cold in personality, more likely to use Style A than B, tall or short, skilled at dressing for success or not, count much less than what leaders stand for, and their ability to communicate ideas and meanings in a manner that inspires, is compelling, and makes the work lives of others more significant. Such concepts as purposing and working to build a shared covenant that bonds people together in pursuit of common values become important. Symbolic leadership and cultural leadership are considered key leadership forces.

In motivation theory the conventional wisdom is that "what gets rewarded gets done." Thus incentives must be part of any managerial strategy or school change initiative. Without incentives, it is believed, people will not be willing to change or otherwise participate as required. In practice, this convention takes the form of leadership bartering, as leaders trade with potential participants something they have for something they want and it works. But leadership by bartering has its limits, too. It results in calculated involvement from people. One complies as long as the exchange continues. When you are no longer getting what you want, you no longer give in return.

On the other hand, when leaders emphasize purposing and covenants, practice takes the form of leadership by bonding. Here, the task of the leader is to create a moral order that bonds both leader and followers to a set of shared values and beliefs. A new wisdom about work motivation and increasing performance emerges: "What is rewarding gets done," and it gets done even when the leader isn't watching, monitoring, or otherwise checking.

The power of calculated involvement pales when compared with the power of moral involvement. Symbols and culture become important concepts in bonding leadership as values are communicated and agreements are struck. People become believers in the school. They view themselves as members of a strong culture that provides them with a sense of personal importance, significance, and work meaningfulness. The result is increased intrinsic satisfaction and greater motivation.

5. Build with canvas

A recent innovation in military technology is a line of folding tanks constructed of canvas, designed to serve as decoys, and designed to create an illusion of strength. Building with canvas is not a bad idea when tinkering with the structure of schooling. For example, one well-established principle in the organization literature is that "form should follow function." Otherwise, the ominous corollary, "if form does not follow function, then function will be modified and shaped to fit the form" will become a reality. "Form should follow function" is good advice and the danger of the corollary (bureaucratizing standards, curriculum, assessment, teaching, and supervision to fit mandated structures or goals) is well known and widespread. We seem not to make much headway in avoiding the corollary. Perhaps this is because we try too hard to follow the principle. But since, on the surface, the principle is not realistic, the corollary wins by default. The way out of this dilemma is to build with canvas.

Take tracking as an example. Some schools adopt tracking policies (function) and then arrange structures (form) to implement them. Change often brings strong and immutable resistance from parents. When this is the case, building in canvas may be the answer. Building in canvas might, for example, leave the tracking structures in place but seek to increase access to honors courses and to use honors' course curriculum and teaching formats in as many regular courses as possible. True, building in canvas in this way may not be as effective as the real thing but if the real thing is beyond our reach at the moment, building in canvas is a doable option. Further, opening up access to the present system of tracking can be an important step in its ultimate demise. At any given time, the prudent leader will choose to keep momentum going toward a goal rather than to engage in a risky win-all or lose-all fight when the odds of losing are so strong.

Thankfully schools have multiple and often conflicting purposes that make exact alignment of structure and purpose difficult if not impossible. This flexibility allows leaders to seek a balance among competing requirements when thinking about how best to organize and structure. Three competing requirements that need balancing are legitimacy, efficiency, and effectiveness.

When organizing for *legitimacy*, schools are responding to the demands and pressures they face from external audiences such as the state, the school board, the corporate sector, citizens groups of various kinds, and accrediting agencies. These audiences require that schools look the way they are "supposed to." To complicate matters, often there are differences among the expectations of various audiences. To obtain legitimacy, the school must be able to communicate a feeling of competence to each of its audiences. In return, it receives needed statements of confidence. More confidence means more support and discretion, and less confidence means less support and more hassles. In general this means that schools must be viewed as well managed, orderly, and safe; adults must be perceived as being in control; events must run smoothly. The flow of schooling must be viewed as familiar to audiences, and this often means not being perceived as too innovative or otherwise too out of pattern. Further, government requirements and legal mandates must be met. However one chooses to operate with respect to the inner structure of schooling, these outer structure requirements will need attention.

Organizing for *efficiency* recognizes that schools are characterized by limited time, money, and human resources. Limited resources must be distributed in a fashion that serves the common good. Tutorials, for example, may be effective ways to organize for teaching, but on a large scale may not be efficient, given our unfortunate commitment to mass education and to staffing patterns of 20–30 students per teacher.

By instilling the value of collegiality among teachers and encouraging flexibility for informal shared teaching, the tutorial concept can be used without the risk of creating and institutionalizing a new organizational structure. Efficiency is an important consideration as school organizational structures are determined. Whatever pattern of organization is chosen, if it does not look efficient, it will not be accepted. Introducing service and internship requirements for students as an answer to a school's quest to make the curriculum more relevant, to give students practical experiences, to teach character, and to achieve other goals frees up teacher time as a bonus. This time can be used by teachers to plan together, to exchange teaching ideas, to try out lessons on one another without adding additional costs or other organizational inefficiencies.

Organizing for *effectiveness* reflects a concern for doing the job of teaching and learning according to agreed-upon specifications and in a manner that reflects competence. Schools are expected, for example, to have a specific curriculum in place, to have definite goals and objectives, and to organize themselves for effective evaluation. Further, certain criteria for schooling considered important by government education departments, accrediting agencies, and educational experts dictate fairly specific organizational and structural requirements.

Because of their relative remoteness, however, external audiences are attracted to the general features of school organizational structure rather than to the details of how these features are to be interpreted and articulated in the day-by-day processes of schooling. Thus, schools are able to exercise a surprising amount of freedom as they interpret policies and rules and implement organizational designs in ways that support sensible teaching and learning.

Schools are in the policy business too. Policies that are handed down from distant sources have to be implemented. In a clockwork world where railroad theories work, there would be a one-to-one correspondence between policies made and policies implemented. But in our world, no close correspondence exists. Implementation decisions lead to the creation of policies in use. Good implementing decisions are able to respond to local contexts and needs by resembling the handed down mandates while being different. When schools build in canvas, they are able to provide the right public face. This gives them the freedom to interpret, decide, and function in ways that make sense. The more effective they are in communicating the right flow of images to external audiences, the freer they are to interpret structures and designs meaningfully for teachers and students, and for learning. The policies that count for students in the end are the policies that are created in use as administrators and teachers practice.

In sum, administrative work resembles an amoeba crossing, and the world of schooling is culturally tight and managerially loose. Practice must reflect these realities if it is going to work. But to have the legitimacy and freedom to practice, we often have to create the illusion that the school is being run like a railroad. For this reason, we sometimes need to build with canvas.

6. Be humble in decision-making

Humble decision-making requires a healthy dose of reflection on one's practice that comes from slow, low-keyed, incremental approaches. In our complex and unpredictable world, these approaches may be more effective than Rambo approaches that combine decisiveness with direct leadership. In humble decision-making leaders are not afraid of trial and error, providing it is focused rather than random (see, for example, Etzioni 1989). They know when to start searching for an effective solution. They check the feedback they are getting at regular intervals and adjust or modify their courses of action, realizing that early decisions made at time one change all the relevant conditions so that subsequent decisions based on the same assumptions may no longer apply. They avoid committing to a course of action too early, preferring instead to commit to revising once underway. Needless to say, they are skeptical of strategic planning frameworks that are too grand in scope and too specific in content.

Etzioni (1989) points out that this humble approach is the logic of decision-making in medicine. Physicians rarely have a personal stake in their treatment decisions. They do, however, have a personal stake in seeking solutions. Thus they are committed to changing treatments as conditions and new evidence warrant. There is nothing Rambo about it and being consistent for the sake of consistency would be considered a serious lapse in judgment.

Etzioni proposes two other features of humble decision-making that can serve leaders well – reasoned procrastination and careful decision staggering. Both challenge the image of the strong decisive leader who stays the course, valuing consistency above all. Both support the folk wisdom implicit in the truism "never make a decision on Friday." Procrastination allows the collection of better information as new options emerge. And procrastination also allows problems to take care of themselves. Decision staggering, by making decisions in small increments rather than going all out like gangbusters, allows for monitoring progress and making adjustments as the process of decision-making moves along. Since these strategies depend on heavy doses of reflection, they benefit from widening the circle of decision-making by including others. A wider circle allows for more ideas to come to bear and for building commitment as decisions are made rather than struggling to get people committed afterwards. Both procrastination and decision staggering increase the quality of what is being decided and the likelihood that decisions will be enthusiastically implemented.

7. Remember moral aspects of leadership

Creating illusions, building with canvas, and practicing humble decision-making raise obvious moral questions in the minds of those not versed in the nature of amoeba crossings. Such ideas are deceptive, one might argue, and have no place in the theory and practice of leadership. Moral questions, however, are not raised by being sensitive to such human realities as loose connectedness, competing preferences and interests, socially constructed reality, and the importance of norms and values. They are raised when we ignore these realities by continuing to push an ill-fitting, rationalistic management theory on school leaders. The consequence of this latter strategy is the constant attempt to shape human nature to fit theory. A more moral and rational strategy for school improvement would be to use a theory that fits human nature better in the first place. It makes more sense to fit the patch to the hole than to move the hole.

Moral questions loom large, nevertheless, as we seek to bring about school changes. Whenever there is an unequal distribution of power between two people, the relationship becomes a

> *"Whenever there is an unequal distribution of power between two people, the relationship becomes a moral one."*

moral one. Leadership involves an offer to control. The follower accepts this offer on the assumption that control will not be exploited. In this sense, leadership is not a right, but a responsibility. Its purpose is not to enhance the leader, but rather the enterprise. Leaders administer to the needs of their school by being of service and providing help. The tests of moral leadership are whether the competence, well-being, and independence of the follower are enhanced as a result of accepting control; and, whether the enterprise benefits.

Leadership combines management know-how with values and ethics. Leadership practice, as a result, is always concerned with both what is effective and what is good; what works and what makes sense; doing things right and doing right things. As school improvement projects are considered and as new organizational designs are implemented, questions of what is good, what makes sense, and what is worth doing deserve equal billing with questions of effectiveness and efficiency. When the two sides of the ledger are in conflict, leaders will be known by the side they emphasize.

Assumptions underlying the amoeba theory

Theories of management and leadership are based on different images of human rationality. Three images are briefly discussed below (Shulman 1989). All three are true to a certain extent, but some are thought to be "more true" than others.

1   Humans are rational; they think and act in a manner consistent with their goals, their self-interest, and what they have been rewarded for. If you wish them to behave in a given way, make the desired behavior clear to them and make it worth their while to engage in it.

2   Humans are limited in their rationality; they can make sense of only a small piece of the world at a time, and they strive to act reasonably with respect to their limited grasp of facts and alternatives. They must, therefore, construct conceptions or definitions of situations rather than passively accept what is presented to them. If you wish them to change, engage them in active problem solving and judgment. Don't just tell them what to do.

3   Humans are rational only when acting together; since individual

reason is so limited, men and women find opportunities to work jointly on important problems, achieving through joint effort what individual reason and capacity could never accomplish. If you want them to change, develop ways in which they can engage in the change process jointly with peers.

The first image – that humans are rational – fits the railroad theory of management very well. Within this theory tracks are laid and stops, timetables, and other predetermined parts of a travel script are provided. We will examine this theory further in Chapter 2. The second and third images, by contrast, are better accommodated by the amoeba theory. Instead of an engineer who drives the train on a scheduled and fixed path to an explicit destination, the leader serves as the nucleus of a cell seeking to bring order, definition, and direction to a mass of protoplasm whose path would otherwise be willy-nilly.

Rationality is achieved by helping people to make sense of their world. As sense builds, limits on rationality are overcome. Sense builds when people are able to construct their own definitions of situations and are involved with the leader in active problem solving. The limits, however, are too great for anyone to go it alone. Thus, one key strategy for sense building is the pooling of human resources in an effort that expands individual reason and capacity to function.

When running the school as a railroad, it is important to emphasize (in order) ends, ways, and means. First, establish your objectives. Then, given your objectives, develop a plan that includes the proper management protocols for obtaining the objectives. Next, marshal your human resources. Prepare them carefully by providing the necessary expectations and direction, appropriate training and development, and the psychological support that will allow teachers and administrators to undertake assigned responsibilities with motivation and commitment.

Ends, ways, and means assume a certain predictability, stability, and rationality that do not always exist in the real world of schooling. Further, this view of planning places too much of the burden for school success on the leader. It becomes the leader's job to set the system up, command compliance, and provide the necessary controls to ensure compliance. Should things not work out as intended, the leader must be held accountable, not teachers, parents, or students.

Unfortunately, because of the rational management biases that exist in our society, the ends, ways, and means system must be in place in the school. But it behoves the leader to build this system with canvas rather than stone. As suggested earlier, a canvas system does not serve as a model for action, but as a source of legitimacy from others who expect the school to look a certain way.

When moving the school as amoeba, one needs to plan in reverse. Without losing sight of the overall vision for the school, the leader first emphasizes means, then moves to ways, and finally to ends. As Hayes points out: "An organization that takes a means-ways-ends approach to strategic planning assumes everybody is responsible for its prosperity. Its success rests on its ability to exploit opportunities as they arise, on its ingenuity, on its capacity to learn, on its determination and persistence" (1985: 118). The emphasis in means-ways-ends is on the development of people, on building their talents and commitments, on linking them to colleagues so that together they are able to accomplish more than alone, on encouraging their minds and hearts and helping their hands.

Once human resources are built up in both skill and heart, the school is better able to acquire and develop new and better ways to function, to create opportunities, and to exploit circumstances in a manner that results in more effective school performance. Because of the unpredictability of the world and the limits of human rationality, it makes sense to emphasize building capabilities of people first, and then encouraging them to develop the ways and means for using their capabilities. This approach is preferred over one that develops plans first and then seeks the know-how and commitment to implement the plans.

Testing the amoeba theory

Let's put the amoeba theory and the other principles of nonorganization described in this chapter to a test.

You have worked with many leaders during the course of your career. Begin by thinking about them. Let them pass through your mind as if you were flipping through the pages of your leadership experiences catalog. Some of the experiences will bring to mind leaders you remember as having been very successful, others as having been unsuccessful, and still other leaders who seemed to have had an indifferent effect.

1 Select the most successful leader you have ever personally encountered. This leader may have:
   - Inspired your spirit and interest.
   - Motivated you to work harder and perform better.
   - Increased your commitment and belief.
     (a) How would you describe this person's leadership style?
     (b) How would you describe this person's "theory" or "philosophy" of management and leadership?
     (c) Give one concrete example that illustrates this person's approach to leadership. (For example, what was the issue? What did the leader do? What were the consequences?)

2 Select the least successful leader you have every personally encountered. This leader may have:
   - Deflated your spirit and interest.
   - Caused you to work less and your performance suffered.
   - Increased your alienation and disbelief.
     (a) How would you describe this person's leadership style?
     (b) How would you describe this person's "theory" or "philosophy" of management and leadership?
     (c) Give one concrete example that illustrates this person's approach to leadership. (For example, what was the issue? What did the leader do? What were the consequences?)

3 Select a leader you personally encountered who would be a prime example of a "nonsuccessful" leader (neither successful nor unsuccessful). This leader may have:
   - Bred indifference with respect to your spirit and interest.
   - Had a nonmotivational effect in the sense that you did what was expected but nothing else.
   - Bred indifference with respect to your commitment and belief.

(a) How would you describe this person's leadership style?

(b) How would you describe this person's "theory" or "philosophy" of management and leadership?

(c) Give one concrete example that illustrates this person's approach to leadership. (For example, what was the issue? What did the leader do? What were the consequences?)

If the theory of leadership and organization I describe in this chapter fits the successful leader better than it does the unsuccessful or nonsuccessful leader, we may have discovered the patch that actually fits the hole that school leaders have to deal with.

Spirit counts too

What are the sources of authority for leadership? On what does a leader base her or his practice? Why should others follow? We usually answer these questions by giving emphasis to a person's expertise, credentials, position in the organization, and interpersonal style. These are, of course, important sources of authority. Leaders cannot do without at least some of them. But rarely are they enough to carry the day in bringing about school improvement. One problem is that these sources are secular. They seek a response from the human mind and hand. But the unique human response is one of spirit, and our spirit responds to values, meaningful ideas, beliefs, moral dimensions, and standards. The character of leadership builds as spirit is tapped. How credible is the leader? Is the leader honest, forthright, and sincere? Does the leader model beliefs, live purposes, exemplify standards? In essence, what does the leader represent, and does this representation symbolize something of value to followers? When this symbolic leadership is emphasized, then the sources of authority for what leaders ask others to do take on moral characteristics – a theme we will pursue further in Chapter 2.

QUESTIONS FOR FURTHER EXPLORATION

1   This chapter is written from the perspective of an American academic.
    To what extent do his ideas have resonance in your own country? – in England? Scotland? Canada? Australia? Hong Kong?, for example.

2   Review the seven principles and rate them on a strongly agree to strongly strongly disagree scale. You might like to use this as a development activity in a leadership workshop or school in-service day.

3   Consider the following matrix. In which quadrant would you place your school?

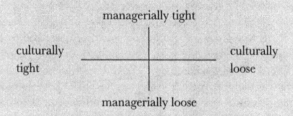

This may provide a useful activity for a school-based workshop. Simply getting to grips with definitions might prove instructive in itself.

2 Leading with ideas

The leadership literature is so vast that superintendents, heads, principals, and teachers are often overwhelmed. Books and journals are filled with theories that tell leaders what to do and how to do it. Most of these theories tell leaders to empower others by delegating, to be considerate of others, to be cheerful, to develop a pleasant climate in the school, to be consistent, persistent, and insistent, and to project a demeanor of calm and support. This emphasis on leadership behaviors and interpersonal qualities can be helpful to leaders. But there are no guarantees that a particular leader will be effective by adopting a recommended approach! Leaders are too different in preferences and personality, and leadership contexts are too different in their scope and contours for leadership to be so neatly packaged. Even if leaders do the same things, the things don't always turn out to have the same effects. No single strategy, style, list, or formula fits all situations the same way. That is why in practice, leadership should be tolerant of many different theories. Lots of differences mean lots of exceptions to any rule that prescribes a one-best way.

Consider, for example, Ogilvey's description of the head chef who ruled the kitchen with an iron hand (cited in McCall and Lombardo 1978). The chef did not tolerate mistakes, inspected every dish, and seldom praised anyone. Most leadership theories would predict the result would be a high level of dissatisfaction in this kitchen and that this dissatisfaction would be accompanied by declines in effectiveness. But, instead, the kitchen was characterized by high levels of *esprit de corps* that "would have done credit to the Marines" (McCall and Lombardo 1978: 159). Two factors seem to cause this turn of events. Both suggest the importance of substance over style in leadership. The chef was the best cook in the brigade and everyone knew it. And, the chef modeled high standards of quality and performance that were infectious. It was not so much what leadership style the chef chose to use, but the chef's recognized competence and the chef's willingness to model the highest standards of performance for the entire kitchen that mattered.

The grammar of leadership

Leadership style and substance, however, need not be separated or antithetical. Style counts when it communicates messages of importance to people and style doesn't count when important messages are not communicated. It sounds like heresy to suggest that sometimes leadership doesn't count in a culture where it is deified, but leadership doesn't count when it is devoid of substance no matter how clever the leader and no matter what style is used. There is, in other words, a grammar to leadership comprised of its phonetics and semantics. Its phonetics is what the leader does and the style used to do it. Its semantics is what this behavior and flair of the leader, and the events that result from their use, mean to others (Pondy 1978). If we focus only on the phonetics of leadership, then an effective leader is one who gets subordinates to do something (usually something that the leader wants done and, if she or he is really clever, in a way that subordinates enjoy doing it). But if we dig deeper and focus on the semantics of leadership then,

> the effectiveness of a leader lies in his ability to make activity meaningful for those in his role set – not to change behavior but to give others a sense of understanding what they are doing, and especially to articulate it so they can communicate about the meaning of their behavior.
>
> (ibid.: 94)

Not deliberately focusing on changing behavior, it appears, is the way to change behavior. Behavior changes once meaning is known and enhanced.

John Gardner (1986a) believes that effective leaders are not only good at dealing with the everyday responsibilities needed to keep a school running, but are also good at dealing with the world of needs, hopes, ideals, and symbols. They serve as models, they enhance the group's identity, and they tell stories that chronicle the group's shared meanings. In his words:

> Any social group, if it is more than a crowd of unrelated strangers, has shared needs, beliefs, aspirations, values, hopes and fears. The group creates norms that tend to control the behavior of its members, and these norms constitute the social order. It is in this context that leaders arise; and it is this context that determines what kinds of leaders will emerge and what will be expected of them. A loyal constituency is won when people, consciously or unconsciously, judge the leader to be capable of solving their problems and meeting their needs, when the leader is seen as symbolizing their norms, and when their image of the leader (whether or not it corresponds to reality) is congruent with their inner environment of myth and legend.
>
> (ibid.: 11)

Admittedly this is an unconventional way to view leadership and many will resist. Some of this resistance comes from having invested too much in current leadership theories. Why, for example, are large schools still being built in North America in the face of overwhelming evidence that portrays the small school as being more effective? The large high school is the product of a theory of leadership and the large high school reinforces this theory. Large schools are staffed by heads and their coterie of assistants and other nonteaching specialists in a fragmented hierarchical arrangement with teachers at the bottom. Teachers advance in rank, money, and influence as they leave the classroom to join this coterie. But in small schools, assistants and non-teaching specialists are rare.

Small schools are more generalist in their stance and more equally staffed. Power is more easily distributed to everyone and exercised by everyone, not just the elites. A change from large to small means a change in the coterie system of school management and that can raise eyebrows (albeit tacit ones) among some who are now in advantaged positions. Abandoning the coterie system, however, doesn't mean less leadership, only different leadership.

Those who have invested too much in our present way of doing things might heed John Steinbeck who wrote, "when a hypothesis is deeply accepted it becomes a growth which only a kind of surgery can amputate" (1962: 180). In this untidy world the choice we have is to live with leadership as a fantasy that looks good, sounds good, but doesn't work, or as an admittedly complex and messy idea that once properly understood can energize both leaders and those they serve. Key to this understanding are the symbolic aspects of leadership.

Emphasizing symbols and meaning

Most leadership theories encourage leaders to practice "situational" leadership. This leadership presumes to carefully calculate behaviors and strategies in a manner that reflects the characteristics of the situations being faced and the psychological needs of the people being led. Calculations are the basis for matching leadership styles to situations and needs. There is some value in thinking about leadership as being situational and it should be practiced as such whenever possible, which isn't often. Given what we get back in return, we give too much attention to the instrumental and behavioral aspects of school leadership and life, and not enough to the symbolic and cultural aspects. This is unfortunate because the symbolic and cultural aspects are more powerful than the instrumental and behavioral aspects in influencing things, in bringing about change, in contributing to effectiveness. And the messier is the context for leadership, the more this is true.

The philosopher Susanne K. Langer reminds us "symbol and meaning make man's world, far more than sensation" (1957: 28). It is in and through symbols that we engage in this world, live our lives, and find meaning. By our very nature we thrive on the construction of meaning. We are suspended in webs of significance that we have spun for ourselves – webs that provide the values, norms, and ways of knowing that make us part of a particular culture (Geertz 1973). Our attempt to understand this culture is an attempt to understand ourselves – a search for meaning. Hanging in the balance is our very existence. In Geertz's words:

> Undirected by culture patterns – organized systems of significant symbols – man's behavior would be virtually ungovernable, a mere chaos of pointless acts and exploding emotions, his experience virtually shapeless. Culture, the accumulated totality of such patterns, is not just an ornament of human existence but – the principal basis of its specificity – an essential condition for it.
>
> (ibid.: 46)

Leadership that counts in a school provides symbols that count and these, in turn, help parents, students, teachers, and others to make sense of their world. Without this sense we invite disorder, disaffection, and disconnection that denies people the hooks they need to latch on to the school, to belong, and to take responsibility for the school's success. Under these conditions, for example, academic engagement of students is difficult if not impossible. The growth and influence of student sub-cultures that are at odds with the school multiply.

Not only are sense and meaning the key to personal satisfaction, they are the key to motivation as well. Teachers and students alike enjoy doing things that are meaningful to them and this circumstance makes a qualitative difference in their lives as learners and teachers. Meaningful learning for students and meaningful work for teachers may be out of fashion in today's world of mandated standards presumed to apply to everyone and of their accompaniments. But savvy leaders know that sense and meaning are necessary to unlock the capacity for people to stretch themselves and for authentic learning to take place. As James Quinn points out: "the role of the leader . . . is one of orchestrator and labeler: taking what can be gotten in the way of action and shaping it – generally after the fact – into lasting commitment to a new strategic direction. In short, he makes meaning" (1981: 59). Thomas B. Greenfield (1984) believed that the purpose of leadership is to create a moral order that binds together leaders and those around them. When leaders seek to add value to their practice they emphasize symbols and meaning.

- How meaningful for you is the work of your school? For your students? How do you come to that judgement?
- What are the symbols that count? What other symbols might be introduced?

The importance of purposing

In the last chapter, we suggested that schools are notoriously loosely connected and that all of the management schemes in the world seem powerless to tighten things up. Karl Weick notes that in schools:

Administrators must be attentive to the "glue" that holds loosely coupled systems together because such forms are just barely systems. In fact, this borderline condition is their strength, in the sense that it allows local adjustment and storage of novel remedies. It is also their point of vulnerability, because such systems can quickly dissolve into anarchy . . . . The effective administrator . . . makes full use of symbol management to tie the system together. People need to be part of sensible projects. Their action becomes richer, more confident, and more satisfying when it is linked with important underlying themes, values, and movements.

(1982: 675)

Emphasizing purposing and cultivating shared values provide the glue that connects people together in meaningful ways. Once purpose and shared values are in place they become compass points and milestones for guiding what is to be done and how. Leaders are then able to help teachers, students, and others to design what to do throughout the school down from these values. Specific goals and purposes remain the responsibility of teachers and others to decide as long as they embody the values.

The providing of purposing to the school is a major aspect of symbolic leadership. Peter Vaill defines purposing as "that continuous stream of actions by an organization's formal leadership which have the effect of inducing clarity, consensus, and commitment regarding the organization's basic purposes" (1984: 91). Key to symbolic leadership is focusing the attention of others on matters of importance to the school. This is done by emphasizing selective attention or the modeling of important goals and behaviors, and by signaling to others what is important and valuable in the school. Touring the school; visiting classrooms; seeking out students and spending time with them; placing educational concerns above management concerns; presiding over rituals, ceremonies, and other important occasions; and providing a unified vision of the school through proper use of words and actions are examples of ways in which symbolic leadership can be practiced.

When leaders are expressing symbolic aspects of leadership, they are working beneath the surface of events seeking to tap deeper meanings and deeper values. Symbolic leadership may be expressed phonetically but it is felt semantically. As Robert J. Starratt (1973) suggests, symbolic leaders identify the roots of meaning and the flow and ebb of daily life in schools so that they can provide students, teachers, and others with a sense of importance, a vision of what is possible, and the substance of purposes that cause them to rise above the seemingly ordinary and mundane. Symbolic leaders are able to see the significance of what a group is doing and, indeed, could be doing. They have a feel for the dramatic possibilities inherent in most situations and are able to get people to go beyond their routines, to break out of the mold into something more lively and vibrant. They use language systems that are easily understood but that also communicate a sense of excitement, originality, and freshness. Above all, the behaviors of symbolic leaders, and the sense and meaning that are communicated from these behaviors, provide a moral framework for the school which enhances purpose and significance.

Ann Lieberman and Lynne Miller, for example, found that heads often practice symbolic leadership as opportunists. In their words:

> When complimenting a teacher for a well-constructed and well-taught lesson, an administrator is making a statement that excellence is recognized and rewarded. When meeting with a teacher whose classroom is in revolt, the principal is expressing concern about what happens behind the closed doors of a classroom and signals a change from previous administrators who have given high marks to a teacher needing improvement. When attending department meetings that focus on curricular issues, the principal is supporting dialogue and informed action. All of these events and actions may be defined as educational leadership – not rational, linear, and planned; but ad hoc, responsive, and realistic. Educational leadership happens, when it happens at all, within the cracks and around the edges of the job as defined and presently constituted.
>
> (1984: 76)

By their actions, statements, and deeds heads communicate moral messages that become a source of authority for what people do. Lieberman and Miller explain:

> Principals [heads] can maintain neutrality and let things progress as they always have; even that is a moral statement. Or they may take an active stance, threatening the assumptions of staff members

and moving a school in more progressive or more regressive directions. Principals condone or condemn certain behaviors and attitudes; they model moral precepts as they go about the job.

(ibid.: 76)

Saphier and King point out that:

> Cultures are built through the everyday business of school life. It is the way business is handled that both forms and reflects the culture . . . . Culture building occurs . . . through the way school people use their educational, human, and technical skills in handling daily events or establishing regular practices.

(1985: 72)

Their point is that it is through routines that heads focus attention, demonstrate commitments, and otherwise "embark on a slow but steady campaign to create a consensus of values and beliefs in a setting" (Dwyer 1989: 22).

Despite the importance and powerfulness of symbolic leadership, most leaders are ambivalent about its use. As James March (1984) points out, they recognize that they spend considerable time trying to sustain beliefs in their schools that communicate to others a certain coherence, importance, and uniqueness which hold their schools in good stead. At the same time, however, they seem to view this sort of activity as being illegitimate or as an imposition on more important things such as making decisions, directing, or coordinating. Yet as March points out:

> Life is not just choice. It is also poetry. We live by the interpretations we make, becoming better or worse through the meanings we impute to events and institutions. Our lives change when our beliefs change. Administrators manage the way the sentiments, expectations, commitments, and faiths of individuals concerned with the organization fit into a structure of social beliefs about organizational life. Administrative theory probably underestimates the significance of this belief structure for effective organizations. As a result, it probably underestimates the extent to which the management of symbols is a part of effective administration. If we want to identify one single way in which

administrators can affect organizations, it is through their effect
on the world views that surround organizational life; those effects
are managed through attention to the ritual and symbolic characteristics of organizations and their administration. Whether we
wish to sustain the system or change it, management is a way of
making a symbolic statement.

(ibid.: 32)

Idea-based leadership

Symbolic leadership can be perverse when its symbols are empty. Empty
symbols lack the substance to communicate the purposes, values, and
ideas that build capacity and commitment among teachers, parents,
and students and help schools to improve. When leadership symbols are
full, by contrast, there is a set of ideas communicated or reinforced that
serves as a source of authority for deciding what should be done in the
school and how it should be done.

Few issues are more important to effective leading than deciding what
will be the reasons why others are being asked to follow. The right decision unleashes a powerful leadership force, a tidal wave, that is able to
bring people together and to point them in a common direction even in
our unpredictable and loosely connected world. The wrong decision
results in a leadership that does not count much (or if it does, not for
very long) and may even be pernicious.

Let's examine our options by asking some questions (see, for example, Sergiovanni 1992: 30–9). Whom should one follow? What should
one follow? Why should one follow? In many schools *whom* means the
leader or one designated by the leader. *What* is the leader's vision or, in
its absence, the school's policies and rules. The *why* question is a bit
fuzzier to handle. Most leaders prefer that no one ask the why question. If an explanation were forced, it might be something like this:
"Follow me because of my position in the school and the system of
roles, expectations, and rules that I represent." This is the simplest and
the most direct way to get things done in schools: rely on bureaucratic authority.

An alternative response might be, "Follow me because I will make it
worthwhile if you do." This is perhaps the most popular way to get
things done in a school: rely on personal authority. Personal authority is

expressed in the form of the head's charisma, motivational abilities, and human relations skills.

Bureaucratic authority exists in the form of mandates, rules, regulations, policies, job descriptions, and expectations that leaders and others communicate. When leaders base their practice on bureaucratic authority, teachers are expected to respond appropriately or face the consequences. When leaders base their practice on personal authority, teachers are supposed to respond to their personality and to the pleasant environment that they provide by behaving appropriately. Teachers then collect the rewards that are made available for this compliance. In both cases teachers respond for calculated reasons. They are motivated to either avoid something unpleasant or to get some reward.

Few readers would advocate a leadership based primarily on bureaucratic authority, but the primacy of leadership based on personal authority remains popular. Leaders like to think of themselves as being good motivators who know how to handle people and know how to get people to do the things that they should by being persuasive in personality or in style. But following a leader because of her or his personality or her or his interpersonal skills is really a poor reason. Teachers, for example, ought to follow their heads not because they are clever manipulators who know which motivational buttons to press, or are pleasant persons who are fun to be with, but because heads stand for something, are persons of substance, and base their practice on ideas.

When purposes are in place and shared values are cultivated, an idea framework evolves in the school that encourages teachers to respond by feeling a sense of obligation to embody these ideas in their behavior. There is, in a sense, a moral authority that emerges which compels them to participate in shared commitments and to be connected to others with whom these commitments are shared.

When personal authority and the authority of shared ideas are compared, which is likely to work best? Perhaps we can find out by playing a thought game. Imagine listening to a speaker whom you admire, enjoy being with, and whose personal style you seek to emulate (this example is inspired by Garry Wills 1994). The topic of her speech, however, is of little interest to you. You simply do not care about the issues she raises and discusses, although you enjoy her manner of presentation. You then listen to a second speaker. You have never met this speaker before and do not care for her style of speaking or for her personality. But you do feel strongly about the issues raised and respond positively to the speaker's ideas.

Given the circumstances above, which of the two persons are you more likely to follow? Which of the two persons is more likely to motivate you to action? If it is the second person, then it appears that admiration, style, and affection may be less important to followership than agreement on ideas, values, and goals. It is useful to think of leadership as having four components: leadership, followership, shared ideas, and action. When leadership is practiced, an interaction takes place between leader and follower, within which ideas and sentiments are exchanged, that leads to something happening. Action, the actual doing of something, is more likely to result from leadership if there is agreement on ideas.

Getting leaders to rely on idea-based leadership is often a hard sell. Heads, for example, like to think of themselves as good motivators who know how to handle people. But following a head because of her or his personality or interpersonal skills is really a poor reason. Teachers ought to follow heads not because they know which motivational buttons to press, but because heads stand for something important – are people of substance and you can see this quality in their leadership practice.

If school leaders commit to ideas as their primary source of authority and make ideas central to their practice, then they are free from worrying so much about all of the behavioral nuances that must be considered under other approaches to leadership. Further, idea-based leadership communicates to teachers that they are respected, autonomous, committed, capable, and morally responsive adults – adult professionals who are able to join with the leader in a common commitment to making things in the school work better for the children.

Three theories for the school

Rules-based and personality-based leadership are embedded in three theories that shape the way we think about school leadership, organization, and management: the Pyramid Theory, the Railroad Theory, and the High Performance Theory.[1]

Pyramid Theory

The Pyramid Theory assumes that the way to control the work of others is to have one person assume responsibility by providing directions, supervision, and inspection. But as the number of people to be supervised increases, and as separate work sites develop, management burdens must be delegated to others and a hierarchical system emerges. Rules and regulations are developed to ensure that all of the managers think and act the same way, and these provide the protocols and guidelines used for planning, organizing, and directing (see, for example, Mintzberg 1979).

While the Pyramid Theory works well for organizations that produce standardized products in uniform ways, it becomes a bureaucratic nightmare when applied in the wrong situation. When applied to schools, for example, Pyramid Theory simplifies and standardizes the work of heads and teachers – and the outcomes reflect this. Standardized practices lead to standardized results for a nonstandardized student body and a nonstandardized world.

Railroad Theory

The Railroad Theory assumes that the way to control the work of people who have different jobs and who work in different locations is by standardizing the work processes. Instead of relying on direct supervision and hierarchical authority, a great deal of time is spent anticipating all the questions and problems that are likely to come up. Then answers and solutions are developed that represent tracks people must follow to get from one goal or outcome to another. Once the tracks are laid, all that needs to be done is to train people how to follow them, and to set up monitoring systems to be sure that they are followed (Mintzberg 1979).

The Railroad Theory works well in jobs that lend themselves to predictability, and where a determination of the "one best way" to do things makes sense. But when the theory is applied to schools, it creates an instructional delivery system in which specific objectives are identified and tightly aligned to an explicit curriculum and a specific method of teaching. Teachers are supervised and evaluated, and students tested, to ensure that the approved curriculum and teaching scripts are being followed. Heads and teachers use fewer skills, and both teacher and student work becomes increasingly standardized. In this theory too, standardized practices lead to standardized results for a nonstandardized student body and a nonstandardized world. Many advocates of standards-based teaching and learning often wind up using the Railroad Theory because they mistakenly believe that standardization and standards are the same thing – a failing of High Performance Theory too.

High Performance Theory

The High Performance Theory differs from the others by de-emphasizing both top-down hierarchies and detailed scripts that tell people what to do. Decentralization is key, with workers empowered to make their own decisions about how to do things. One gets control by connecting people to outcomes rather than rules or work scripts. Borrowing from the practices of efficient business organizations, the High Performance Theory assumes that the key to effective leadership is to connect workers tightly to ends, but only loosely to means (see, for example, Peters and Waterman 1982).

When the High Performance Theory is applied to schools, the ends are measurable learning outcomes usually stated as standards. Though outcomes themselves are standardized, schools are free to decide how they are going to achieve them. Heads and teachers can organize schools and teach in ways that they think will best enable them to meet the standards. High Performance Theory emphasizes collecting data to determine how well workers are doing, and to improve the likelihood that standardized outcomes specified by distant authorities are met. Again, standardized practices lead to standardized results for a nonstandardized student body and a nonstandardized world. The issue isn't standards. Standards can be a good thing. The issue is that standards are standardized. And to get this kind of uniformity they have to be set by distant authorities rather than by students, teachers, schools, and local communities – a topic discussed further in Chapter 5.

While the Pyramid, Railroad, and High Performance Theories provide understandings that can help us make better decisions about school leadership, they also share features that make their systematic application to schools inappropriate. In all three theories, schools are perceived as formal organizations, like corporations or transportation systems. But the formal organization metaphor does not fit very well the nature of a school's purposes, the work that it does, the relationships needed for serving parents and students, the context of teachers' work, or the nature of effective teaching and learning environments.

Both the Pyramid and Railroad Theories, for example, separate the planning of how work will be done from its actual performance. "Managers" (state and other distant authorities) are responsible for planning *what* will be done and *how* it will be done. "Workers" (heads, teachers, and students) are responsible for *doing*. This separation of what and how from doing may work in running a chain of fast-food restaurants, but not for schools where professional discretion is essential to success.

In High Performance Theory, workers are provided with outcomes and other standards, and then get to decide how to do the work. But because planning what to do is separated from planning how to do it, problems of isolation, fragmentation, and loss of meaning remain. When means and ends are separated, not only is professional discretion compromised, but so are democratic principles. Few parents, heads, teachers, or students are likely to feel empowered by being involved in decision-making processes that are limited to issues of how, but not what – of means but not ends. Further, the ends wind up driving the means anyway. A one-best list of standards for everyone assessed by the usual high stakes tests inevitably drives the curriculum, how time is spent, and even how teachers teach.

The school as a moral community

Many school leaders don't ignore the three theories but don't put much stock in them either. Instead, they view schools as moral communities and struggle to make this view a reality. Moral community has two important advantages over the other theories: it provides for moral connections among teachers, heads, parents, and students, and it advocates helping all of them to become self-managing.

All theories of leadership emphasize connecting people to each other and to their work. These connections satisfy the needs for coordination and commitment that any enterprise must meet to be successful. The work of teachers, for example, must fit together in some sensible way for school purposes to be realized, and teachers must be motivated to do whatever is necessary in order to make this connection. But not all theories emphasize the same kinds of connections. The Pyramid, Railroad, and High Performance Theories emphasize contractual connections and assume that people are primarily motivated by self-interest. To get things done, extrinsic or intrinsic rewards are traded for compliance, and penalties for noncompliance. Leadership inevitably takes the form of bartering between the leader and the led.

Moral connections are stronger than the connections that come from extrinsic or intrinsic rewards. Moral connections are grounded in cultural norms rather than in psychological needs. "A norm . . . is an idea in the minds of the members of a group, an idea that can be put in the form of a statement specifying what the members . . . should do, ought to do, are expected to do, under given circumstances" (Homans 1950: 123). A norm is a norm only when not following it leads to some kind of sanction or penalty. Usually this penalty takes the form of feeling uneasy when we are not meeting commitments or when important others are disappointed with what we are doing.

> *"Moral connections are stronger than the connections that come from extrinsic or intrinsic rewards."*

With leadership firmly grounded in shared ideals, and with moral connections in place, heads, teachers, parents, and students can come together in a shared followership. The leader serves as head follower by leading the discussion about what is worth following and by modeling, teaching, and helping others to become better followers. When this happens, the emphasis changes from direct leadership based on rules and personality, to a different kind of leadership based on stewardship and service.

The secret

The secret both to successfully practicing idea-based leadership and to helping schools become moral communities is to replace communication with conversation. Conversation may not be able to move mountains, but it can get teachers, citizens, state officials, and other stakeholders to think differently, to join together in a union of mutual responsibility, and to make good decisions together for children.

Unlike communication, which is the unilateral transmission of information from one person to another and which reflects our bureaucratic–hierarchical culture of schooling, conversation invites the reciprocal exchange of ideas (Interfaith Education Fund 1998). Since conversation is relational and reciprocal, it requires a commitment to mutuality. Mutuality implies the sharing of power with, by, and among people regardless of their level or role in a way that recognizes the dignity of each, and to sustain this sharing (Nothwehr 1998). In the educational world, for example, states count, but not more than do parents, teachers, students, and others. Heads count too. And the more that heads practice mutuality by engaging in conversation with others, the more they count. Conversation is the way to bring people together, to build needed capacity, and to win the commitment needed from everyone to make the school work well.

Reflecting on your practice

Howard Gardner (1995) believes that the ultimate impact of the leader depends on the stories that he or she communicates to others. Sometimes the story line emerges as a result of conversations with teachers and then is adopted by the leader, who acts as the spokesperson and standard bearer for the ideas. Some leaders have story lines themed to caring, every student can learn given the right conditions, teacher learning is key to a school's success, parents are essential partners in teaching and learning, a focus on authentic learning is fundamental, or the basics come first. Other leaders have story lines with different themes. If the leader is effective, then her or his stories become the school's stories, providing the sense of identity and coherence that holds things together as the school struggles to make its stories a reality. To Gardner leadership is much more cognitively oriented than most presume. In his words:

> Confronted with the phenomenon of leadership, a cognitively oriented . . . [approach] is likely to ask such questions as, What are the ideas (or stories) of the leader? How have they developed? How are they communicated, understood, and misunderstood? How do they interact with other stories, especially competing counterstories that have already drenched the consciousness of audience members? How do key ideas (or stories) affect the thoughts, feelings, and behaviors of other individuals?
>
> (ibid.: 16)

It is now time for us to examine our own leadership and the stories we communicate to others by its use. If those with whom you work and for whom you have responsibility were asked to comment on your leadership by responding to the following questions: What are your ideas for the school? How have they developed over the last few years? How are they communicated to faculty, students, and parents and how are they understood or misunderstood? How do your stories interact with other stories? How do your stories affect the thoughts, feelings, and behavior of faculty, students, and parents? What would they say in response? Start by answering the first few questions now, but make it a point to respond to all of the questions in the next day or two. Write your responses out and share them with a trusted colleague who knows your work pretty well. After getting feedback from this colleague, try answering this question: If you were to examine what is actually going on in your school, how you spend time, what you actually communicate by word and deed, would there be a correspondence between what you have written and the stories one could infer from your actual behavior? Don't be discouraged if the answer is no, not always. The stories we believe in and espouse are not always the stories that we live. But the first step to increasing the correspondence between one and the other is knowing what the stories in your heart are and how close you are to realizing them in the messages you communicate to others.

Skeptics might ask: But where is the real leadership? Real leadership, they would argue, comes from stating specific objectives, developing strategies, and getting measurable results. Beliefs are too subjective and too soft to have real currency in accounting for leadership. John Gardner would reply:

> Humans are believing animals. They have religious beliefs. They hold to one or another political doctrine. They have beliefs that supply meaning in their lives, beliefs that tell them how to conduct themselves, beliefs that console. The leader who understands those beliefs and acts in terms of that understanding has tapped a source of power. If the system of ideas is deeply embedded in the culture it can play a significant role in legitimizing leaders and in validating their acts.

(1986b: 9)

QUESTIONS FOR FURTHER EXPLORATION

1   Lieberman and Miller are quoted as saying that "It is within the cracks and around the edges" that leadership may be found.
    What relevance would this have for you in your school?
2   If you were asked to describe, "the belief system" in your school, how would you reply?
3   Leadership conveys an implicit followership message. How, for your school, would you complete the sentence, "Follow me because . . ."?
4   Pyramids and railroads have been used as metaphors.
    What kind of metaphor would you choose to describe the system you would like to work in?
5   How do notions of "stewardship" and "service" translate into the day-to-day reality of school life at the sharp end?
6   What is the "leadership story" in your school?
    Who tells it? Are there different stories?

3 New leadership, roles, and competencies

What kind of leadership will be needed for schools to effectively serve society as we look further into the future? Whatever the answer, it will not be the superhero leadership of the past. The new century will not be kind to leaders who seek to change things by the sheer force of their personality. Nor will it be kind to leaders who seek to change things by the sheer force of their bureaucratic authority. Instead, we will need leadership for schools themed to learning, to the development of civic virtue, and to the cultivation of self-management.

In this new leadership, leaders will spend much more of their time on purposing, developing idea structures for their schools, building a shared followership, and helping their schools become communities of responsibility. This change in the way we do things will influence corporations and other kinds of organizations as well. Warren Bennis, the noted business theorist, puts it this way: "Most urgent projects require the coordinated contributions of many talented people working together. Whether the task is building a global business or discovering the mysteries of the human brain, it does not happen at the top" (Bennis cited in Byrne 1999: 90).

But a change in our practice requires a change in our thinking. Our leadership practice cannot be separated from its underlying theories. Leadership is distinctly normative, reflecting our values, beliefs, and assumptions.

Being normative doesn't make leadership less rigorous, scientific, or legitimate as long as we make sure that our view of leadership and the values that drive it are made known to parents, students, and teachers. This public disclosure is critical to ensure that our practice remains

Unquestionably, there is value in charting and understanding what we can call the *hand of leadership*; some behaviors do seem to make more sense, in certain circumstances, than others do. But the hand alone is not powerful enough to account for what leadership is; indeed, it may not represent leadership at all. If we want to understand . . . any . . . leader's behavior, we have to examine the *heart* and the *head* of leadership, too.

The heart of leadership has to do with what a person believes, values, dreams about, and is committed to – the person's *personal vision*, to use the popular term. But it is more than vision. It is the person's interior world, which becomes the foundation of her or his reality.

The head of leadership has to do with the mindscapes, or theories of practice, that leaders develop over time, and with their ability, in light of these theories, to reflect on the situations they face. Reflection, combined with personal vision and an internal system of values, becomes the basis of leadership strategies and actions. If the heart and the head are separated from the hand, then the leader's actions, decisions, and behaviors cannot be understood.

The head of leadership is shaped by the heart and drives the hand; in turn, reflections on decisions and actions affirm or reshape the heart and the head. This interaction can be depicted as follows:

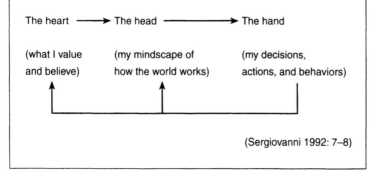

(Sergiovanni 1992: 7–8)

ethical and wins the respect of people whether they agree with us or not. Still, not all views are equal and not all views will be viable as we move into the twenty-first century. That is why debating views of leadership is a worthy exercise. Different views mean different practices. And since leadership continues to be important in determining whether a school will work well for teaching and learning or not, different practices of leadership mean different levels of school effectiveness. Having said that, it is no easy task to identify a single view of leadership that beats all other views all of the time. Probably each of the following meanings for leadership have roles to play:

MEANINGS FOR LEADERSHIP

- Leadership means influencing parents, teachers, and students to follow the leader's vision (see, for example, Bennis and Nanus 1985 on visionary leadership).
- Leadership means influencing parents, teachers, and students to identify, understand, and find solutions to the problems that they face (see, for example, Heifetz 1994 on learning and problem-solving leadership).
- Leadership means not only pursuing useful goals that meet the needs of parents, teachers, and students, but goals that elevate them to a higher moral level (see, for example, Burns 1978 on transformational leadership).
- Leadership means enhancing purpose, meaning, and significance that parents, teachers, and students experience by serving shared ideas and ideals (see, for example, Sergiovanni 1992 on moral leadership).
- Leadership means being practical by selecting means to achieve purposes that take into account the loosely connected, messy, and generally nonlinear characteristics of schools (see, for example, Cohen and March 1974 on educational organizations as organized anarchies).

Though all five meanings of leadership are important and can contribute to the enhancement of teaching and learning, the first meaning – to follow the leader's vision – raises some concerns. "Follow me" leadership seems more appropriate to the twentieth than the twenty-first century. Nonetheless there are legitimate occasions when that is what should be done. Heads, for example, have some responsibilities and obligations that require a definition of leadership heavily weighted in their favor. Further, there are occasions when the head's wisdom and experience are so superior and the consequences of error are so great that the head's view of leadership should legitimately dominate. Moreover, there are occasions when heads use follow me leadership and lay out the vision in such a way that symbolic meanings are communicated that enhance meaning and significance. Remember, for example, that chef described in Chapter 2 who ran the kitchen with an iron hand. But for schools to work effectively over the long haul, the other meanings of leadership need to dominate.

Visions cannot be routinely mandated by bureaucratic authority or routinely inspired by personal style. Instead they need to be discovered or forged as a *consequence* of everyone learning, problem solving, striving to reach a higher moral level of operation, and finding sense and meaning in the bargain. Linda Lambert and her colleagues (1995), for example, define leadership as involving a reciprocal process that enables members of a school community to construct meanings that lead to common purposes. This constructing of meaning is less a role to be assumed by some, but more a role to be assumed by all. This process, Lambert suggests, promotes learning and encourages a collective responsibility for the school (Lambert 1998).

Leadership and change

We often think about change when talking about leadership. For many the two are simply different sides of the same coin.[1] Change is thought to be good and resistance to change is thought to be bad. Leaders are considered successful if change succeeds and unsuccessful if change does not succeed. It seems not to make much difference what the substance of this change is. All of us know, for example, of heads who are considered highly effective, not because they have improved their schools, but because they have changed their schools.

It is hard to figure out just where the problem starts – with our understanding of leadership or with our understanding of change. One thing seems clear – regardless of where the problem starts, it ends in the same place. Much of our thinking about leadership and about change is vacuous. We are so concerned with process that we neglect substance. We spend so much time and effort trying to figure out the right strategies for leadership and change that we give only scant attention to why we are leading and changing, to what is the content of our strategies, to whether and how they influence teaching and learning.

It is not just school leaders who are enamored with process but researchers and educational policy makers too. Policy scientists, for example, find themselves absorbed in struggling to figure out the best methods to get teachers and schools to change. Is whole school change better than changing only part of the school? Is it better for teachers to be convinced that a change is good before they try it? Or will their attitudes change once they are required to use the proposed changes in their practice? How do change agents provide the ways and means needed for teachers to be successful once they do try a proposed change? Will incentives motivate teachers to change? Should incentives be individually based or school based? If a school adopts restructuring model A, will they be better in getting student test scores up than if they had adopted model B? What about the role of leadership? What approach, style, or strategy of leadership is most effective in getting teachers and schools to change in the way it is thought they should? How do you "reculture" a school? Do you start with a vision or discover your vision a little later? Does school size make it easier to succeed at change? What about teacher learning? Is it better to concentrate on teacher learning than to concentrate on changing organizational structures? How do the findings that lower class size seems to be related to higher test scores fit into the picture? What schools have been able to put several features of "successful change" into practice at the same time? What do these schools look like? Can we transplant these findings to other schools? How can these findings about change become policies? What are the best ways to implement these policies so that schools and leaders within them will do what they are supposed to?

It is taken for granted by everyone (or so it seems) that schools and school programs are effective when changed, without struggling with the adequacy of the definition of effectiveness used. What works is the focus. Few seem interested in what would happen if the definition of effectiveness were to change from A to B. Let's face it, some ideas are not worth advancing. We would be better off if certain change attempts failed rather than succeeded. We would be better off if some heads knew less about the change process than they do. When ideas are not worth advancing, less effective leadership may be a virtue and teachers who resist change may be heroes.

Consider some further examples. Is a school that commits itself to teacher learning as the focus of its change strategy successful if it changes from a "let's help our students learn to use their minds well" kind of place to a "let's go for the high test scores by narrowing the curriculum, learning how to implement alignment strategies, and emphasizing test-taking skills" kind of place? Is a school successful in change if it restructures by requiring all teachers to adopt a particular school design, even though 20 percent of the teachers oppose the change and parents and students have had no say in the decision? Is a school that motivates teachers with cash incentives, or coerces them by posting the scores of the children they teach in the local newspaper, successful if teachers are now involved in their work for calculated reasons rather than professional or moral reasons? Is a school that changes from a thinking curriculum to a basic skills curriculum in math and science successful because students achieve higher scores on aligned assessments even if they understand less? If one listens carefully to the conversations of policy makers as they propose changes, it would be hard not to conclude that the answer to these questions is "yes." Further, the change strategies used to reach a particular goal (i.e. a thinking curriculum) may be the same ones used to reach a rival goal (a basic skills curriculum), providing further evidence of the vacuousness of a process approach to leadership and change. In both cases if the change is successfully implemented, victory is declared by the change agents involved even if teachers, students, and their families are the losers.

The glory and the praise

Why is it so common for process to be placed over substance in the leadership and change literature, particularly that literature which emanates from North America? I think there are two reasons. One reason is that the North American leadership literature itself is biased toward change. There is glory to be had by leaders who are successful in bringing about change, even if that change turns out not to be a good idea. Thomas Sowell captures this idea cogently in the following comment:

A quarter of a century before the Gettysburg Address, Abraham Lincoln gave another important but lesser known speech, pointing out that the basic free institutions of American society were already in place – and therefore would provide no glory to leaders who merely preserve them. Glory would be won only by changing these institutions, whether for the better or the worse.

(1999: 5B)

While this zest for change in North America cannot be matched by most other places, this sentiment will, I wager, bring sympathetic nods from people elsewhere.

James Lipham (1964) was one of the early writers in educational administration to make the distinction between management and leadership by claiming that leadership was about changing things while management was about running things as they are. In his words, leadership is "the initiation of a new structure or procedure for accomplishing an organization's goals and objectives or for changing an organization's goals and objectives" (p. 122). Upping the stakes a bit, the noted leadership expert, Warren Bennis, noted that while managers do things right, leaders do right things (Bennis and Nanus 1985: 21). The former implies stability and the latter change. Given these definitions, which would you rather be? A "manager" who focuses on maintaining organizational systems or a "leader" who focuses on changing organizational systems?

> *"Which would you rather be? A 'manager' who focuses on maintaining organizational systems or a 'leader' who focuses on changing organizational systems?"*

Equating leadership with change is an idea that finds its way deep into the educational literature. In today's world it is the leader as change agent who gets the glory and the praise. But leadership should be regarded as a force that not only changes, but protects and intensifies a school's *present* idea structure in a way that enhances meaning and significance for students, parents, teachers, and other locals in the school community (Sergiovanni 1984). This enhancement provides a sense of purpose, builds a culture, and provides the community connections necessary for one to know who she or he is, to relate to others, and to belong. Think of leadership force as the strength or energy brought to bear on a situation to start or stop motion or change. Leadership forces are the means available not only to bring about changes needed to improve schools, but to protect and preserve things that are valued. Good heads, for example, are just as willing to stand firm and to resist change as they are to move forward and to embrace change. It all depends on whether the change being considered is good. Good change, I propose, advances teaching and learning in a manner that is consistent with the values and culture of those being served by the school without compromising larger intents in the form of standards for decency, civility, fairness, and other civic virtues.

The dominance of technocracy over democracy

The second reason why substance is typically subordinate to process in both leadership and change is because, too often, democracy is subordinate to technocracy. In much of the world, for example, the school is at the same time a democratic institution driven by the needs and desires of students, teachers, and parents at the local level and a technocratic institution in the form of a governmental–corporate complex driven by technocratic elites at the state and federal levels. As a democratic institution, deep and meaningful participation at the local level is valued. As a technocratic institution, reliance is placed on technical experts who engage in "policy-science" that decides for everyone what our standards are, what the outcomes of schools should be, how schools should pursue these outcomes, how these outcomes should be assessed, who the winners and losers are, and what the consequences of this winning and losing will be. In a sense this dual world of schooling pits local participation and democratic politics against technical expertise; parents, teachers, and students against distant government and corporate elites.

Though both democratic and technocratic can play important roles if properly brought together, too often the democratic side of school life is dominated by the technocratic. In a society based on technical expertness and governmental corporatism, the roles of public opinion, local teacher expertness, student voice, and citizen participation are viewed as romantic oddities. Democratic values are thought not to be sufficiently responsive to the new "world class" standards and to the higher levels of achievement defined by these standards. Standards, it is presumed, are needed to catapult a community, state, or nation into the midst of economic competition as a successful player. The answer to this perplexing problem is not to pit one of these impulses against the other but to bring the two together in a way that technocratic virtues serve democratic ends.

Choosing a strategy

Virtually everyone agrees that improving the academic, developmental, and civic lives of teachers and children in schools is an important purpose. Where we disagree is how to achieve this goal. Whatever else leadership is, it involves choosing strategies to achieve purposes and since strategies are contested, leadership remains complex and controversial.

Let's dig a little deeper. What options do we have when choosing a strategy? One popular option is to use *mandates* that specify in detail what the minimum standards, expectations, and rules are and that provide the management systems necessary to ensure that schools comply with these mandates (see, for example, L. M. McDonnell and R. F. Elmore 1987). Mandates usually are accompanied by close monitoring and include penalties for noncompliance. A related option is to rely on *incentives* that trade rewards for compliance. But, like so many other common practices, these twentieth-century approaches to leadership have only limited

---

MANDATES AND INCENTIVES

- Create uniformity.
- Reduce variation.
- Stifle creativity.
- Focus attention on minimums.
- Lead to calculated involvement.
- Encourage maximization of self-interest.

Mandates and incentives, used excessively, are capital poor by lacking the ability to produce future value as conditions change.

roles to play in the future. Mandates and incentives come up short because they create uniformity, reduce variation, stifle creativity, focus our attention on minimums, lead to calculated involvement, and encourage the maximization of self-interest at the expense of the common good. Mandates and incentives are *capital poor* – lacking the ability to produce future value on behalf of students, their parents, the local community, and the state.

Two alternative policy strategies can help provide the leadership we need: capacity building and grassroots democratic participation. Both, as we shall discuss below, are *capital rich* by being able to produce future value on a continuous basis. Both expand value as demand expands, change value as expectations change, and create new value as new school requirements for learning emerge.

Capacity building as a capital idea

It seems strange to be talking about capital and expanding value – terms borrowed from economics. But economic concepts and terms are used regularly by policy elites as they address school reform issues and it makes sense for us to figure them out and see what we can learn and use. Capital, for example, takes human and organizational forms as well as economic. At root, capital refers to the value of something that when properly invested produces more of that thing, which then increases overall value. Leaders in learning communities, for example, generate capital that increases the value of teaching and learning and increases the quality of student behavior and academic performance – themes we will examine in Chapter 4, "Leading Communities of Responsibility."

But developing capital is not that simple. Leaders in schools that function more like formal organizations than communities (see, for example, Sergiovanni 1994a) generate capital too, and this capital can also be helpful to teachers and students. The difference is in the kind of capital that is generated. Organization-like schools are efficient generators of management, physical, fiscal, and other forms of *material* capital. Communities, by contrast, are efficient developers of social, academic, intellectual, professional, and other forms of *human* capital.

Both material and human capital can add value to teaching and learning. Material capital provides the structures and resources that can make the work of teaching and learning easier. But the literature is full of examples of schools where levels of material capital are low yet levels of student performance, development, and civility are high. By contrast, I can think of no instance where levels of social, academic, intellectual, and professional capital are low and student performance is high (with the obvious exception being when students bring all the capital they need for success with them to school).

> "*I can think of no instance where levels of social, academic, intellectual, and professional capital are low and student performance is high*"

Capacity building creates intellectual capital by emphasizing the development of knowledge, competence, and skill of parents, teachers, and other locals in the school community. As parents and other citizens are able to provide the support that students need to belong and to be successful at school, they get smarter, and smarter parents mean smarter students. Teacher development can help build the intellectual capital that teachers need to keep up by increasing their knowledge of the disciplines and the pedagogical-content knowledge teachers need to teach these disciplines effectively.

But intellectual capital is more than what we know and more than what one group knows collectively. Intellectual material not only has to be developed and captured, but formalized and put to work if higher value assets are to be produced.

> Intelligence becomes an asset when some useful order is created out of free-floating brain power – that is, when it is given coherent form . . .; when it is captured in a way that allows it to be described, shared, and exploited; and when it can be deployed to do something that could not be done if it remained scattered around like so many coins in a gutter. Intellectual capital is packaged useful information.
>
> (Stewart 1997: 67)

Leadership for learning, therefore, is not just about developing and gathering what people know, but packaging it into frameworks that are useful in enhancing school practice.

We still have to go further because knowing what to do and how to do it is not enough. Local capacity needs to be put to work to actually improve schools. This is where democratic participation comes in. Encouraging and developing grassroots democratic participation harnesses the capacity of locals, enhances sense and meaning, and builds community connections. These are examples of the social capital needed to support high levels of authentic leadership and learning in schools.

Local capacity does not just happen, but must be developed as a matter of policy. The only way to beat the complexity, uncertainty, and continuous change that schools face and still maintain order is by creating local communities of responsibility that are able to cultivate higher levels of disciplined self-management among students, teachers, heads, parents, and other members of the local school community. This disciplined self-management is expressed as locals take more responsibility for their own learning by monitoring and managing their own performance. But, as Hackman (1986) suggests, self-managing teams are not likely to flourish unless communities of responsibility also function as self-designing teams. Self-designing teams have the responsibility and the discretion to decide their own organizational structures and learning environments. And finally, self-designing teams are not likely to flourish unless communities of responsibility also function as self-governing teams. Self-governing teams have considerable autonomy in setting a fair share of their own purposes and directions, in defining their own responsibilities, and in deciding how these goals will be pursued.

Local capacity remains undeveloped, however, as long as the policy process itself – the ends of schooling, not just the means – is determined by the excessive use of mandates and incentives as the primary strategy for change and as the primary focus of leadership – a lesson not yet learned by leaders who seek to enhance local autonomy while at the same time mandating uniform standards and assessments.

Policy strategies and leadership roles

Figure 3.1 shows how local leadership roles change as the emphasis shifts away from mandates and incentives and toward capacity building and democratic participation:

• When mandates are the prime means to bring about change the leader as *manager* dominates. The leader emphasizes aligning school goals with management systems, controls, and assessments that ensure achievement.

- When incentives are the prime means to bring about change the leader as *motivator* dominates. The leader emphasizes trading rewards for compliance as social contracts with parents, teachers, and other locals are struck and enforced.
- When capacity building is the prime means for bringing about change the leader as *developer* dominates. The leader emphasizes learning that builds the capacity of parents, teachers, and other locals to function more effectively.
- When grassroots democratic participation is the prime means to bring about change the leader as *community builder* dominates. The leader emphasizes identifying shared values and ideals, standards, and purposes that provide a moral source of authority for how people treat each other, for the decisions that are made, and for how they behave as these concerns are embodied in the daily life of the school.

As capacity building and democratic participation are emphasized, leaders focus less on managerial and motivational roles and more on developer and community builder roles. The reverse relationship is also

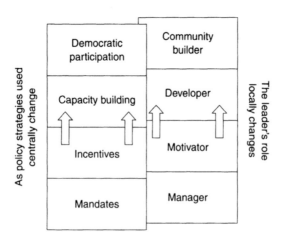

Figure 3.1 How central strategies influence local leadership.

true. Emphasizing mandates and incentives forces leadership away from developing capacity and building strong communities of learning. toward twentieth-century manager and motivator roles.

Competencies for leadership

How do changes in roles affect heads? They will have to master seven basic competencies in order to lead effectively: the management of attention, the management of meaning, the management of trust, and the management of self (Bennis 1989), as well as the management of paradox, the management of effectiveness, and the management of commitment.

---

7 BASIC COMPETENCIES

The management of:

1   attention;
2   meaning;
3   trust;
4   self;
5   paradox;
6   effectiveness;
7   commitment.

The management of attention is the ability to focus others on values, ideas, goals, and purposes that bring people together and that provide a rationale, a source of authority for what goes on in the school. Leaders manage attention by what they say, what they reward, how they spend time, the behaviors they emphasize, and the reasons they give for decisions they make. They practice purposing, defined as that continuous stream of action that induces clarity, consensus, and commitment regarding the schools' purposes (Vaill 1984).

The management of meaning is the ability to connect teachers, parents, and students to the school in such a way that they find their lives useful, sensible, and valued. Even the seemingly mundane routines of schools are valued and are connected to the larger purposes and meanings that define who people are, why they are in the school, why the school needs them, and why their participation with the school is worthwhile. Together the management of attention and the management of meaning answer the questions: What are our priorities? What are our commitments to each other? Why are they important? How do they link to the ordinary things that we do? These messages help people become connected to each other and to the school, building hope and commitment, and raising levels of civility and academic engagement.

The management of trust is the ability to be viewed as credible, legitimate, and honest. Bennis (1989) uses the term "constancy" (p. 21) to communicate that whether parents, teachers, or students like what a head does or not, they always know where that head is coming from, what she or he stands for, and why she or he is doing things. It is not enough to make decisions; leaders have to explain them and show how they are linked to the heart and soul of the school as well.

The management of self is the ability of heads to know who they are, what they believe, and why they do the things they do. When a head's behavior can be defended in such a way that others at least understand and at least respect that behavior, then self-knowledge has been achieved. The management of self is a sleeper of sorts. Few experts in leadership recognize its importance. Perhaps this is because lots of heads seem to have the needed self-knowledge. Yet they remain unremarkable as leaders. The trick is for leaders to combine knowledge of their values with the ability to defend them without offending others.

The management of self is an art worth developing – but one not easily achieved without a measure of practical intelligence. Practical intelligence is the ability to know how things work and to make things work. The cultivation of keen insight into human nature and the putting together of this knowledge in some useful way are examples. Robert Sternberg illustrates practical intelligence by telling the story of Jack, the "smartest" student in the class, and Jim who was often the butt of Jack's jokes. Jack routinely offered Jim the choice of a nickel or a dime. To Jack's delight, Jim always selected the nickel. When asked why, Jim said that if he chose the dime Jack would no longer ask him to choose. "I've collected over a dollar so far [;] all I have to do is keep choosing the nickel" (Sternberg 1996).

The management of paradox is the ability to bring together ideas that seem to be at odds with each other. Bringing together an emphasis on rigorous standards without imposing standardization or compromising local discretion; expecting a great deal from teachers while empowering them to take control of their professional lives; responding to adolescent needs for independence while providing the disciplined safe havens they need; involving parents without compromising professional autonomy; and bringing everyone together in a common quest united by shared values while honoring diversity and promoting innovative ideas are examples. When implemented, these seemingly contradictory ideas can actually bring us together, make us brighter and stronger, and help us to achieve larger purposes. The management of paradox is easier when leaders look to ideas, values, and visions of the common good as a moral source of authority for what they do and when they know the difference between *power over* and *power to*. They distribute power widely with the understanding that its purpose is to achieve goals rather than to control others. They consider themselves successful when good things happen, regardless of who is responsible. Thus, they have no vested interest in control-oriented management – preferring goal oriented.

The management of effectiveness is the ability to focus on the development of capacity in a school that allows it to improve performance over time. Key to the management of effectiveness is how school success is understood and measured. When effectiveness is managed well, school success involves getting *results* and more. School success also involves *learning* and cultivating *relationships*. Learning builds the capacity of teachers to know more about their work, to figure out how to create better pathways to success, and to improve their practice as a result. Relationships provide the support that teachers need to come together as a community of practice.

In the language of economics, if we want to increase human capital (results) we have to pay attention to developing intellectual capital (learning) and social capital (relationships) in the school as well. Thus determining success of any initiative requires answers to three sets of questions:

---

3 QUESTIONS

1   What are we accomplishing? Are our results of high quality? Does what we are doing make sense to parents and other constituencies?
2   What are we learning about our work? Are we likely to be more effective the next time around as a result? How are we sharing what we are learning?
3   How are we working together as a community of practice? Are we supporting each other and helping each other? Are we proud of what we are doing and do we enjoy working together?

The management of commitment provides the overall framework for leadership practice as the other six competencies are implemented. The management of commitment involves moving leadership away from bureaucratic and personal factors toward cognitive factors – toward ideas (see Chapter 2). As this happens moral authority begins to replace bureaucratic and personal authority. Moral authority comes from each school's sense of the common good and the promises and obligations that good requires from everyone. Idea-based leadership calls on everyone – teachers, parents, and students – to join the leader in accepting responsibility for what happens in the school. As ideas and common commitments are shared, so is leadership.

The transformation of leadership to ideas and the sharing of control broadly throughout the school are ways to be responsive while being orderly; to be predictable in an unpredictable world; to continuously build capacity and to ensure future academic success. As this transformation takes place, leadership becomes more local, more important, more powerful, more creative, more responsive, and more successful in bringing people from different levels of the educational system together to improve schools.

Some rules that might help

This chapter began with an invitation to readers to join together and dream a bit about the possibilities of leadership. It is now time to focus this discussion more clearly in light of the nonrational world of schooling. It remains that superhero images of leadership will not work. And it remains that mandates and incentives are not powerful enough to function as engines that will drive our efforts to improve schools. Both are handicapped by a tendency to create uniformity, reduce variation, stifle creativity, focus on minimums, encourage self-interest, and lead to calculated involvement in an age when the virtues needed to survive and flourish are exactly opposite. In tomorrow's world success will depend upon the ability of leaders to harness the capacity of locals, to enhance sense and meaning, and, as we shall discuss in Chapter 4, to build communities of responsibility.

What needs refocusing is an honest look at how leaders will be able to work toward their ideals in a world of schooling where paradox is routine. The last of the five meanings of leadership proposed at the beginning of this chapter was as follows:

> Leadership means being practical by selecting means to achieve purposes that take into account the loosely connected, messy and generally nonlinear characteristics of schools.

In the 1970s Cohen, March, and Olsen (1972) characterized educational organizations as "organized anarchies." They justified this label by pointing out that the goals of such organizations are difficult to specify with precision, constantly changing, varying from one part of the school to another, and in other ways problematic. They pointed out further that the technology of schooling was unclear. Although we know how to start up a school and how to staff it, we don't understand very well how it works. And moreover, participation in schools is so fluid (at least for the students who are served and often for the faculty as well) that it remains perpetually unstable. The flow of students coming and going requires constant reculturing of the school with variable results. As a way to survive this unpredictable environment, people are inclined to look out for themselves rather than each other or the school. Behavior based on self-interests becomes the norm and these interests are pursued by playing politics (see, for example, ibid.).

Given these conditions of organized anarchy, how do leaders successfully implement the leadership competencies discussed above? Carefully, I suppose. But we can go further than that. Cohen and March

(1974) provide a number of tactical rules that leaders can use as they seek to influence the course of decisions in their schools (see, for example, 195–229). Several of these rules are summarized below:

TACTICAL RULES

Rule 1 is to spend time. Decisions that influence what happens in a school take lots of energy and energy is a scarce resource. Whoever is willing and able to invest energy by devoting the time needed in making decisions and in forwarding proposals has a considerable claim on the decisions that get made and the proposals that get accepted. Combine this with the reality that most people in schools have vast zones of indifference – are just plain not interested in most of the things that are happening in their schools – and the claim is enlarged. Most teachers, for example, care deeply about matters that affect their classrooms and their own teaching lives. The further away are issues from the classroom, the less likely are these teachers to be interested. Whoever is disinterested forfeits her or his claim on what is going on. I may not, for example, like a particular decision that has been made in the school. But, having not invested the time needed to research the issue and to discuss it in any meaningful way, I really can't complain much about that decision.

Rule 2 is to persist. It is a mistake to presume that if what you propose is not accepted today, it will not be accepted tomorrow. Given the flow of participation in most schools the people who are interested or able to be involved today may not be the same ones that are interested or involved tomorrow. You simply deal with different individuals even though the issue remains the same. As Cohen and March (1974) put it: "The specific combination of sentiments and people that is associated with a specific choice opportunity is partly fortuitous. . . The loser who spends his time weeping rather than reintroducing his claim will persistently have something to weep about" (p. 224).

Rule 3 is to exchange status for substance. Instead of worrying about how credits are allocated for good ideas and about whether one's own position in the school is being enhanced or not, heads should focus their attention on proposed changes and other issues of substance remembering to gladly distribute the credit for ideas and their success to others.

Rule 4 is to facilitate opponents' participation. The sure-fire way to win over opposition is to give them a piece of the action by involving (indeed needing) their participation and absorbing their ideas in one form or another in the proposal, being considered. As ideas are absorbed into a proposal, so are the people.

Rule 5 is to provide garbage cans. Think of the arena for decision-making as a garbage can. Various school problems and solutions are deposited in this can, though typically solutions are only loosely connected to problems. Now the odds of making decisions joined to a solution are doubled because not only are solutions matched to problems but problems are matched to solutions as well.

While matching solutions to problems may be okay in today's schools, one has to be surreptitious about matching problems to solutions. We can learn much from the behavior of our students. Recall the time when a group of students came to your office to complain about the noise and disorder in the cafeteria. Remember the committee of students and faculty you appointed to study the issue? They recommended that a jukebox be installed in the cafeteria as a way to provide a focus and absorb the attention of the students. But what was the problem anyway? The students, you see, wanted that jukebox all along but didn't want to request it for fear you would say no. So, they invented a problem that you would find attractive and that would lead to the acceptance of their solution. Though the problem followed the solution, it appeared to everyone that the solution followed the problem and that made it legitimate.

If you can think of some other rules, please pass them on. Leadership in schools is tough enough to practice without everyone pitching in and helping each other. In the next chapter we turn our attention to building and leading communities of responsibility.

QUESTIONS FOR FURTHER EXPLORATION

1   Change is not intrinsically a good thing. It depends on the substance of change. In the changes you are currently experiencing what are the substantive issues you agree with? What aspects of change are you uncomfortable with? Are these issues discussed in your school?

2   In your experience what leadership strategies are most effective in getting people to change?

3   Five rules of tactical leadership are suggested in this chapter. You are invited to provide a sixth. What would it be?

4   Consider ways in which you might use the five tactical rules as a workshop activity in your school.

5   This chapter poses a question "Why is it so common for process to be placed over substance in the leadership and change literature?" What is the answer?

4 Leading communities of responsibility

The image of school as community is important and can be used by heads to help make our schools more caring and productive places for both teachers and students. In this chapter I argue that not only should we commit ourselves to this image but we should strive to make schools *communities of responsibility*. This strategy is not only good in itself, but is the best pathway to school effectiveness. The idea of community can be validated in research and argued thoughtfully. But rarely are these enough. Most of us have pretty strong ideas about what is the nature of human nature and about what organizational characteristics are important to schools. These ideas color our thinking about community. Even in the light of research and other "hard" evidence, our feelings spring from the personal theories we hold about what is important and good for individuals and what is important and good about their relationships with each other and society.

For example, below are three statements that can be used to assess some of your own personal theories. For each statement award up to 10 points to indicate the extent to which you believe the statement is true. If you believe the statement is absolutely true, award it 10 points. If you believe the statement is absolutely false, award it no points. If you believe the statement is somewhere in between, choose a number between 1 and 9 that best reflects your feelings. Start with the first two statements, ignoring the third statement for the moment:

1   You believe in an image of a society of individuals who are armed with rights but who, by comparison, are free from externally imposed responsibilities. You view any social formulation of the common good with suspicion. Instead, you believe that the common good is defined as each individual person pursues her or his self-interest. Freedom and the rights that go along with it are bounded only by not interfering with the rights and freedoms of others. Privacy is an absolute value. You believe that attempts to scrutinize behavior, to check up on what is going on, or to otherwise impose centralized accountability systems thwart individual rights and compromise freedom.

2   You believe in an image of a society of highly disciplined individuals who are subject to a standard code or rule of law which embodies an official definition of the common good. This code is determined through representative government that operates centrally. You believe in freedom that is bounded by this code. Once the common good is defined, you believe that central authorities are responsible for holding people accountable. Individual privacy is secondary to societal scrutiny as this code is enforced and as this good is pursued.

My guess is that you felt a little uncomfortable with awarding too many points to either of the two views. You probably stayed within a 3–6 range in awarding points. If I am right, then you may be a candidate for a third view of individuals and society – one with a communitarian bent (see, for example, Etzioni 1993, 1999). This view is reflected in the third statement. How many points would you award to this statement?:

3   You believe in a balanced view of society that provides an alternative to both the view that each person should be free to form and pursue her or his own vision of the common good and to the view that centralized representative government

should define and enforce a vision of the common good. This alternative encourages the development of *communities of responsibility* within which the social formulation of the common good is, in a large measure, decided locally by individual communities. Once this good is defined by the local community, central authorities are responsible for ensuring accountability. This accountability should be in the form of scrutiny by fellow members of the community and by neighbors from other communities. Scrutiny by fellow members and by neighbors, coupled with public disclosure, provides the accountability that makes direct control by central authorities less necessary.

This chapter explores schools as communities of responsibility and examines how such schools are led. Community is viewed as a moral phenomenon rather than simply a geographic or territorial entity. Communities share many common characteristics. They spring from common understandings that provide members with a sense of identity, belonging, and involvement that results in the creation of a tightly held web of meaningful relationships with moral overtones. Communities of responsibility not only fit this description, but go beyond by building into their cultures a capacity for self-regulation that ensures both internal and external accountability. Not only do members of the community share a common focus, they also feel morally obliged to embody this focus in their behavior.

Communities of responsibility are not easy to cultivate in schools. But once established they become powerful substitutes for the bureaucratic and personally based leadership that seems now to dominate the school scene. Leadership is defined, in part, by its source of authority – a concept introduced in Chapter 2. We noted that the source of authority for bureaucratic leadership is the position power of the leader. And the source of authority for personal leadership is the personality and motivational skill of the leader. When personal leadership is used, it is presumed that we are primarily motivated by self-interest. Thus, we can be easily seduced into following the leader if the leader uses the right personality, style, and interpersonal skill to provide the psychological and material rewards we want in exchange for our compliance. In both bureaucratically and personally based leadership the rule is "follow me," either because my leadership position allows me to make your life miserable if you don't or my leadership ability allows me to make your life pleasant if you do.

In communities of responsibility, by contrast, leadership is based on a different kind of authority – one, embedded in ideas, that encourages us to respond from within; to become self-managing. Instead of follow me, the emphasis is on following commitments, promises, obligations, validated research, sound principles, agreed upon standards, and other ideas. Chapter 2 referred to this source of authority as leading with ideas.

In communities of responsibility it is norms, values, beliefs, purposes, goals, standards, hopes, and dreams that provide the ideas for a morally based leadership. These ideas are not mandated scripts that require carbon-copy conformity. They are, instead, more like frameworks that function as compasses which provide people with a heightened sense of understanding, meaning, and significance. As a result, plenty of room exists for diversity to be expressed and celebrated in the life of the school – a topic that will be explored further later in this chapter. When leadership is morally based, its effect on spirit, commitment, and results is not only strong but obligatory, allowing the school to function as a community of responsibility

Why is community so important in schools? Five reasons stand out:

---

5 REASONS FOR COMMUNITY

1 community helps satisfy the need that teachers, parents, and students have to be connected to each other and to the school;
2 community helps everyone in the school to focus on the common good;
3 community provides students with a safe harbor in a stormy sea – a place where they are accepted unconditionally;
4 community supports learning; and
5 community builds relationships and responsibilities.

When accompanied by a strong commitment to learning and when accompanied by steps that demonstrate this commitment to students (both are indicators of academic press as described by Sebring and Bryk 1996; and Shouse 1996)[1], then being responsive to community leads to improved student performance. Further, providing for the connections needs of teachers, parents, and students, and focusing on the common good lead to improved student behavior, stronger bonds of collegiality among the faculty, and more productive relationships with parents.

Cultural connections

Connections are particularly important to building community. Community is something most of us want in order to experience the sense and meaning that we need in our lives. We cannot go it alone. We have to be connected somehow, somewhere. Being connected to others and being connected to institutions we value is a way to become connected to ourselves; to know that we belong; to know that we count for something; to know that we are valued. Community is a particularly important source of connection for children and young adults. If the connections needs of our students are not met by the school, they look elsewhere for community and even create it for themselves. Too often the results are not very pleasant. Students forming cliques that insulate them from other students and students joining gangs and other antisocial groups are examples.

But not all of the connections we might make available to students count the same way. Not all connections are community oriented. Some connections are *rational* and other connections are *cultural*. Rational connections are based primarily on the pursuit of self-interest and involve trades. When we choose rational connections, it is assumed that motivation results from logically weighing options and selecting the one that gives us the most benefits at the least cost. In the corporate world, for example, employers agree to provide their employees with certain economic benefits and other amenities. In return employees agree to follow job rules and to meet job expectations. Similar bargains are struck in the sports world and in other sectors of our formal society.

Though each of the parties to this kind of social contract offers the other connections, the offers are conditional. If I don't like the deal (say the video which the teacher promises I can watch if I behave) or if I don't believe the deal offers a fair exchange for what I am contributing to the bargain ("You mean all I get is to watch a video if I behave?"), I weaken my connections by not playing along. If the teacher is unhappy with my contributions to the deal, she or he responds similarly by weakening connections from the other side. This emphasis on rational trades, and the calculated involvement it typically causes, is the nature of contracts. It is the way bargains work.

Cultural connections, by contrast, are more covenantal than contractual. They are bargains all right, but bargains of the heart and soul. They are based primarily on loyalties, purposes, and sentiments that emerge from stated and unstated understandings and commitments that obligate people to each other and that obligate people to the institutions they value. Covenants are more than agreements. They are promises. Promises play an important role in our lives. Promises among people and between people and valued institutions, for example, imply certain mutually held actions and commitments that are considered obligatory. Unlike legal documents that spell out all the technical details, however, covenants are planted within the hearts of people, bind people together morally, and obligate them morally, to the conditions of the covenant (Jeremiah 31: 33). Cultural connections and covenantal relationships are the foundational pillars of communities of responsibility.

Social contracts, Sacks (1997) argues, are maintained by the likelihood of gain or the threat of loss. Social covenants are maintained by loyalty, fidelity, kinship, sense of identity, obligation, duty, responsibility, and reciprocity. Social contracts are common in the worlds of commerce and politics where organizations are more formal, impersonal, and objective. Social covenants are common in "families, communities, traditions, and voluntary associations" (ibid.: 16). These familial groupings of people and purposes make up the world of communities.

How simple it would be if this were an either–or situation. But most of us belong to formal organizations and to community-like enterprises at the same time. Both the rational and cultural connections and both the social contracts and social covenants are important parts of our reality. We seek to be autonomous and to belong. We crave independence and we crave connections. There are times when we vigorously pursue our own self-interests and there are times when we give unselfishly of ourselves to the common good.

What about schools? Like most individuals, schools should have features of both formal organizations and communities programmed into their DNA. Both social contracts and social covenants have a place. But one should not cancel out the other. Let's experiment a little:

AN EXPERIMENT

Make a list of 30 enterprises found in London, Singapore, Melbourne, New York, Vancouver, or some other large city. Now arrange the enterprises in your list along a continuum from the most community-like (the family would be an example) to the most formal organization-like (perhaps Xerox or some other large corporation). Assuming that roughly half of the enterprises you listed were community-like and the other half were organization-like, where would you place the school on this continuum?

My guess is that you would place the school on the community side of your continuum, but not so deeply into that side that the school would wind up next to the family. Give or take two or three places, my guess is that you placed the school in the middle of the community side of your continuum. This is probably a reasonable and realistic position for the school – solidly on the community side of the continuum, but not so deeply that objective, rational and instrumental benefits of formal organizations are not able to be tapped and used by the school.

In today's world the problem is not getting the school too close to the family. It is getting the school on the community side of the continuum in the first place. Though our children need community-like schools, too often they find themselves in schools that are too organization-like. When this happens, we run the risk of students becoming disconnected from schools with negative consequences for learning. Families, too, need community-like schools if they are to participate in the powerful ways needed for them to help their children learn (Henderson and Berla 1994). And, I believe, our teachers need community-like schools too if they are to practice their craft fully.

Community and diversity

Bonding and bridging (Putnam 2000) are ways in which schools can provide the community connections that students and their teachers need. Bonding connections looked inward and tilted toward exclusion, while bridging connections looked outward and tilted toward inclusion. It is possible for schools that are becoming bonding communities to be so concerned with developing common frameworks that commonness becomes synonymous with sameness. Should this happen, then the strong norms of community may well coerce everyone to think alike and be alike as the price of admission. Community as the antidote to connections problems in society, then, becomes the poison (Sergiovanni 1992: 141). This possibility is not likely to occur, however, when community is authentic. Community has many meanings. But at root it is the Latin *communis* and the Latin *communitas* that provide the themes for defining authentic community. *Communis* means common and *communitas* means fellowship. Thus, say Carey and Frohnen:

> a true community, one that lives up to its name, is one in which members share something in common – something important enough to give rise to fellowship or friendship and to sustain it. There may be many kinds of communities with varying ends or goals. But each must form around characteristics, experiences, practices, and beliefs that are important enough to bind the members to one another, such that they are willing to sacrifice for one another as "fellows" or sharers of a common fate.
>
> (1998: 1–2)

Communis and *communitas* make the membership of a community as a whole more than the sum of its individual members.

When individuals (students, teachers, parents) are bound to shared ideas, values, beliefs, and frameworks, bonds of fellowship emerge that provide a moral climate which empowers the membership as a whole. In schools this fellowship has two dimensions: a sense of collegiality among faculty that resembles a community of practice and an Aristotelian view of leadership that involves a moral commitment to care for and nurture one's colleagues. For students, the image is a learning community characterized by high levels of caring and civility and of cooperative learning.

Aristotle (1962) argues that the motives for fellowship can be pleasantness, usefulness, or goodness. Community members enjoy each other, find association with each other to be mutually beneficial, and feel morally obliged to accept and look after each other. Though all three motives may be present in *communitas*, fellowship cannot exist in an authentic sense without the moral motive. Durkheim cites Rousseau to make this point. A community is:

> a moral entity having specific qualities distinct from those of the individual beings which compose it, somewhat as chemical compounds have properties that they owe to none of their elements. If the aggregation resulting from these vague relationships really formed a social body, there would be a kind of common sensorium that would outlive the correspondence of all the parts. Public good and evil would not be merely the sum of individual good and evil, as in a simple aggregation, but would lie in the relationship that unites them. It would be greater than that sum, and public well-being would not be the result of the happiness of individuals, but rather its source.
>
> (Durkheim 1960: 82)

The last phrase of Rousseau's quote, that public well-being is the source of happiness and not the result, makes another point. Communities embody civic virtue – the willingness of individuals to sacrifice their self-interests on behalf of the common good. And this virtue is the reason why communities are so powerful in uniting parents, teachers, and students in common

> *"Communities embody civic virtue – the willingness of individuals to sacrifice their self-interests on behalf of the common good."*

purpose. This common purpose provides the focus that contributes to school effectiveness (see, for example, Bryk and Driscoll 1988; Hill, Foster and Gendler 1990; Hill and Celio 1998; Sergiovanni 1994a, 2000).

Protecting individualism while maintaining community

Protecting individualism while maintaining community may, at first blush, seem like a paradox. But the importance of civic virtue and of the *communitas* nature of communities are the individual's insurance policy against coercive communities that seek to impose narrow idea structures on the unwilling. They are the guarantors of diversity. For individuals to band together in fellowship and friendship, the ideas that first bind them must be freely accepted. Let's take respect as a common value, for example. While respect may not be negotiable once established as a value, there are many ways to show it. This latitude increases the likelihood that the value of respect will be freely accepted and will contribute to fellowship. Rigor is another example. While rigorous standards may exist, they need not be the same for everyone. Students may demonstrate rigor in different ways – again increasing the likelihood that the value will be freely accepted. In these examples respect and rigor are values held in *communis* but shared in *communitas*. *Communitas* is the antidote to "group think" in other ways as well. Together *communis* and *communitas* combine unity and diversity in such a way that not only does each persist, but each is enhanced by the other. The philosopher Mary Rousseau explains the challenge of this paradox of community as follows:

> To put the challenge in terms of human relationships, a philosophy of community must validate the dream of every human heart. That dream is that we might love and be loved, that we might associate with each other, in such a way that closeness and autonomy both survive, and even enhance each other. In our dream, someone – everyone – accepts us, affirms us, praises us, enjoys us just for being who we are. We are recognized as unique and uniquely valuable individuals, encouraged to be ourselves to the utmost, loved in our totality and for our own sakes. And yet, the love that encourages our uniqueness and autonomy brings the warmth and security of total belonging . . . In our dream, closeness does not threaten independence but enhances it – and *vice versa*. Those with whom we are most intimate leave us free to be ourselves. We have our cake and eat it too. We belong but are not possessed. We are free but not alone.
>
> (1991: 4)

Key in solving the paradox of community is the concept of altruistic love and how it is different than egocentric love. Both are ties that bind people together in community ways but only one achieves authentic community. Egocentric love views relationships between and among people in terms of self-interest and self-gratification. For example, Robert may be devoted to members of his weight-loss group and together they establish a high level of community based on mutual goals and shared fellowship. But they are together because they need each other to lose weight. The motive for *communitas*, in this case, is usefulness not goodness. Once Robert loses weight, his interests in the group are satisfied and he is likely to leave the group. Despite the close relationships enjoyed while Robert was getting something out of his ties with the group, three months later he has difficulty even remembering the names of most of the members.

Altruistic love, by contrast, results in ties that bind through hell and high water. Robbie joined with others in the spirit of *communis* and *communitas* to form a neighborhood hospitality group. She believed in the group's purpose and was benevolently concerned about the members of the hospitality group and the newcomers to the neighborhood. She was involved because she thought this was the right thing to do. Her love for her work and for the people she worked with and served was not motivated by selfishness, but by her desire to do something she thought was important. She stuck with it even when she did not particularly like some of the newcomers. To her, loving someone in this altruistic sense was more important than just liking them. To love meant to help, to serve, to be in communion with others. Altruistic love provides the fellowship that allows – even encourages – people to be different and still be accepted.

There is a message here for heads. The virtues of serving, caring, respecting, empowering, and helping without asking for anything in return are far more powerful "motivational devices" than is the artful manipulation of motivational science that seeks to trade need fulfillment for compliance. The altruistic love modeled in those virtues builds the kind of *communis* and *communitas* that not only binds teachers together as colleagues and fellows, but binds them to obligations and commitments as well. This binding compels them to rise to the occasion and do their best. Egocentric love, by contrast, involves little more than a trading session that leads to loose ties at best and calculated ties at worst. In Mary Rousseau's words:

Since community, moral goodness, and our existential fulfillment all coincide, we can now see the important second sense in which love is the tie that binds. . . . We are bound, in the sense of being obliged, to love, to do what is morally right, to enact community. In other words, community is not an option for us. It is an obligation, a categorical moral obligation, one that we cannot escape. Community is our basic moral absolute, not a matter of preference or a value that is relative to time, place or circumstances. . . . It is something that we ought to do no matter what, something that we simply must, in all conditions, strive for. The basis for this binding power is the fact of our existence in the community of being.

(1991: 115)

The box entitled "How common should *communis* be?" links this discussion to the concepts of bonding and bridging connections. *Communis* and *communitas* are the means to finding the right balance between bonding and bridging. Sharing a common framework of values themed to trusting relationships and the development of a culture of respect in schools allows for bringing together a commitment to both the common good and individual expression. Borrowing from Etzioni (1996/97) I use the metaphor "mosaic" to show how bonding and bridging connections can be brought together.

HOW COMMON SHOULD *COMMUNIS* BE?

Communities need not and should not be built upon all encompassing, narrowly defined, carbon-copy norms but on norms of caring and collaboration. Collaborative cultures share common beliefs in the value of both the individual and the group (Nias, Southworth, and Yeomans 1989).

The distinguished sociologist Amitai Etzioni (1995) offers "principled decentralization" as an antidote to possible divisions that might exist among different communities within the same school. Localized communities can be developed in such a way that they embody a responsibility to encourage a variety of different voices and interests, not as isolated entities, but within a larger sphere of a pragmatic coalition built around common goals and ideas where an overlapping consensus has been established and bounded by a framework of mutual respect.

Etzioni (1996/97) offers the metaphor mosaic as a way to imagine how this bounded autonomy might work. A mosaic is comprised of a variety of elements of different shapes and colors that are held together by a common frame and glue. It symbolizes a society in which various communities maintain their cultural particulars while, at the same time, recognizing that they are integral parts of a more encompassing whole. Within this image, communities have firm commitments to both their uniqueness and their shared framework. And, community members have layered loyalties in the form of allegiance to two different dimensions of the whole (Etzioni 1996/97).

Eight conditions seem necessary for community theory to evolve in schools in this direction:

1   Schools need to be redefined as collections of people and ideas rather than remain defined by brick and mortar. Thus within any school building many independent and semi-independent schools might exist side by side.

2   Shared values that lead to the development of tightly knit communities of mind and heart need to be encouraged within schools while, at the same time, respect for the defining differences that make a school unique need to be encouraged between schools. The goal should be to create communities nested within communities, neighborhoods within cities, schools within schools across the educational landscape.

3   Whether they are functioning as schools within schools or as free standing schools connected to a larger complex of schools, all schools need to be tied together by common foundational values, by frame and glue to hold everything together.

4   Layered loyalties to one's own school community and to the larger community of schools need to be cultivated.

5   Nothing in the concepts of nested communities, neighborhoods within a city or schools within a school should

compromise the individual rights that students, parents, teachers, and other community members enjoy as part of a commitment to democratic values.

6　This emphasis on individual rights needs to be tempered by deliberately linking rights to responsibilities within a framework of commitment to civic virtue, defined as the willingness of each member of the community, individually and collectively, to sacrifice their self-interest on behalf of the common good.

7　Within practical limits, students and their families, as well as teachers, should be able to choose the particular school, school family or school within a school they wish to join. This "school" of choice should be part of a larger legal framework of school or schools and resourced at an equitable level.

8　Commitment to both individual rights and shared responsibilities that are connected to the common good should provide the basis for moral leadership.

> T. J. Sergiovanni, "The Elementary School as Community in a Diverse Society," The William Charles McMillan III Lecture, Grosse Point Academy, 10 March 1999

The learning community

Leadership in the learning community has a special meaning that comes from the word pedagogy. Most of us view pedagogy as simply the process of teaching. But derived from the Greek, pedagogy means teaching and leading. Leading involves caring, helping, guiding, and serving in ways that can only be accomplished when the pedagogue is willing to function *in loco parentis*. The pedagogue leads by accompanying the child and living with the child in a way that provides direction and care. As van Manen explains: "Here, take my hand!" "Come, I shall show you the world. The way into a world, my world, and yours. I know something about being a child, because I have been there, where you are now. I was young once" (1991: 38). The part of caring that is unique in the learning community is the formal emphasis the community gives to providing students with authentic learning experiences that train and expand the mind as well as the body and soul.

Unfortunately, considering students as clients and considering students as customers does not help. Whether we intend it or not, "client" has a technical ring to it that suggests teaching and learning are about delivery – the delivery of expert services to customers who are dependent on our expertise. Since delivery is so different from leading, it distances teachers from their roles as pedagogues and reduces them to roles as technicians. Having been distanced themselves, students assume little or no responsibility in this image for the success of teaching and learning. Success rests entirely on the teacher's shoulders. This technical ring is so loud that we tend not to focus on the primary definition of client as one who is dependent on another and as a result, fail to emphasize the moral obligations that bind teacher and student together in the process of learning. The "customer" metaphor raises even greater problems. Customers are interested in the services they receive. When you and I are in this role, we try to maximize our self-interest and show little or no loyalty to the "vendors" who are providing us with services.

As we think about the roles of students in communities, the image of citizen may make more sense. Like customers, citizens have rights and make demands too. But citizens also have responsibilities. Citizenship implies a measure of personal sacrifice, a measure of fidelity, and a measure of obligation to help make the school work. For these reasons we need to call on students to be citizens of the school and to call on them to participate in its work and play as citizens. Let's face it, as Banner and Cannon point out: "that pair sitting on the seesaw are equally responsible to each other. If the student gets up and leaves, the teacher falls to the ground" (1999: 60). They believe that students need to be fully engaged in the struggle to learn and that this involves "reaching inside themselves, by learning to summon what is naturally theirs – whether it's their enthusiasm for a subject, their curiosity, imagination, or aspiration" (ibid.: 60).

Playing the ability game

Taking responsibility for one's own learning is tough enough under ideal conditions, but virtually impossible when we ask students to play the ability game of learning rather than the task game of learning.

When we ask students to play the ability game of learning, we ask them to outperform others. When we ask children to play the task game of learning, we ask them to master tasks that are challenging and interesting (Ames 1984, 1992; Maehr and Midgley 1996).

Midgley and Wood (1993) point out that when playing the ability game, students come to believe that demonstrating ability is the school's main goal and that how they stand relative to others is the measure of their success. This perception comes to permeate the school's culture affecting what is believed, valued, and done. When playing the task game, by contrast, students "come to understand that what is valued is mastery, hard work, taking on challenging tasks, and making academic progress. Competition and comparison with peers are discouraged" (p. 249). In this culture the emphasis is on the development of ability rather than the demonstration of ability. How one is doing relative to her or his goals rather than relative to others is the measure of success.

Midgley and Wood use the example of teaching your child to ride a bike to illustrate the difference:

> If we're trying to teach a child to ride a bike, we don't say, "Your sister learned to ride more quickly," or "You're doing an average job of learning how to ride this bike." Instead, we say, "Hang on; pedal faster." In other words, we focus the child on figuring out how to do the task and not on how he or she compares with other kids.
>
> (ibid.: 250)

Reclaiming trust

Establishing schools as communities of responsibility is a way in which schools can reclaim the trust of central governments and the general public – something I believe everyone wants and needs. Many of the standards-driven and high-stakes accountability systems for schools now in place across the globe are there because state governments do not trust local teachers and administrators, local citizens and local governments. In the USA, for example, governors and state level policy makers do not believe local schools can be trusted to make the best decisions for the children they serve. Locals, they feel, are either unwilling or unable (and sometimes both) to set high and rigorous standards so the state had better do it for them. Further, locals cannot be trusted to hold themselves accountable for getting results so the state had better do that for them too.

But, as Etzioni points out, "higher levels of communal scrutiny facilitate compliance better than higher levels of public [governmental] control and often allow that control to be kept at a lower level" (1999: 214). He advocates scrutiny not by governments but by members of the community itself and by members of disinterested neighboring communities. In his words, "the best way to curtail the need for governmental control and intrusion is to have somewhat less privacy" (ibid.: 213). With scrutiny and public disclosure at the local levels comes trust and with trust comes more local control. In the next chapter, I propose that scrutiny by the larger community in the form of periodic, widely publicized school quality reviews (SQR) conducted by members of the local community and by disinterested parents, teachers, and citizens from neighboring communities is a viable way to hold schools accountable without compromising the benefits of local control.

QUESTIONS FOR FURTHER EXPLORATION

1 Professional autonomy is highly valued by teachers. But working for the *common* good is seen as one of the hallmarks of the moral community. How can effective leadership reconcile these tensions?

2 What do you see as the role of the student in your school? – Customer? Client? Consumer? Collaborator? Co-producer? Creator?

3 Do teachers in your school feel a genuine sense of accountability? To whom? For what? Expressed in what way? With what consequences?

4 Have schools lost the trust of:
The public at large?
Parents?
Policy makers?
Students?
If so, for any of these groups, how might trust be re-established?

5 School character, school effectiveness, and layered standards

As the formation of character is central to the role of education, so is the cultivation of organizational character central to the role of school leadership. Thinking about school character is not much different from thinking about individual character. When we think of individuals with character, our thoughts point to their integrity, reliability, fortitude, sense of purpose, steadiness, and unique qualities of style and substance that distinguish these persons from others. Substance, distinctive qualities, and moral underpinnings are particularly important. Leaders with character anchor their practice in ideas, values, and commitments, bring to their practice distinctive qualities of style and substance, and are morally diligent in advancing the integrity of the schools they lead (see, for example, Sergiovanni 2000).

Similarly, schools with character are unique in important ways. These schools know who they are, have developed a common understanding of their purposes, and have faith in their ability to celebrate this uniqueness as a powerful way to achieve their goals. Key to the success of schools with character is for their parents, students, and teachers to have control over their own destinies and to have developed norms and approaches for realizing their goals. Both control and distinctiveness distinguish schools with character from schools where character is less developed. Both control and distinctiveness enhance sense of purpose, identity, and meaning for organizational participants. A school has character when there is consistency between *that* school's purposes, values, and needs, and its decisions and actions. A school without purposes of its own, without a sense of how to achieve those purposes, and without homegrown commitments to those purposes places its character at risk. This risk increases when excessive mandated standards and assessments from afar replace a school's unique goals and purposes. Finding the right balance between legitimate mandates and school autonomy is an important condition for organizational character to flourish. This theme will be taken up in the next section as we consider the role lifeworlds play in school effectiveness.

> *"A school has character when there is consistency between that school's purposes, values, and needs, and its decisions and actions."*

School character builds when certain virtues are incorporated into its culture. Fullinwider divides the virtues into four groups: "(1) the moral virtues – honesty, truthfulness, decency, courage, justice; (2) the intellectual virtues – thoughtfulness, strength of mind, curiosity; (3) the communal virtues – neighborliness, charity, self-support, helpfulness, cooperativeness, respect for others; (4) the political virtues – commitment to the common good, respect for law, responsible participation" (1986: 6). The virtues provide a framework for looking ahead and providing leadership and for looking back to take stock and evaluate progress. And the virtues provide a sense of direction and confidence that can help schools navigate a safe passage through stormy seas.

The lifeworld of schools

Why is a unique sense of what a school stands for and a unique commitment to this sense so important? Because these qualities help to protect and grow a school's *lifeworld*. Borrowing from the philosopher and sociologist Jürgen Habermas (1987), we might think of the lifeworld as a school's local values, traditions, meanings, and purposes. In the best of circumstances the lifeworld determines what local strategies and initiatives will be used by schools to achieve their own destiny (Sergiovanni 2000). The lifeworld includes the traditions, rituals, and norms that define a school's culture. Lifeworlds differ as we move from school to school and these differences lay the groundwork for developing a school's unique character. As character builds, the capacity of a school to serve the intellectual, social, cultural, and civic needs of its students and of its community increases.

School character is also important because it is linked to effectiveness. School effectiveness can be broadly defined as achieving higher levels of pedagogical thoughtfulness, developing relationships characterized by caring and civility, and achieving increases in the quality of student performance as measured by traditional tests and alternative assessments. The relationship between school character and this definition of school effectiveness has been well documented (see, for example, Bryk and Driscoll 1988; and Hill, Foster and Gendler 1990). The bottom line is that character adds value to a school by contributing to the development of various forms of human capital. Two particularly important forms of human capital are social capital and academic capital.

Social capital consists of norms, obligations, and trusts that are generated by caring relationships among people in a school, community, neighborhood, or society (Coleman 1988, 1990). When students have access to the social capital they need in school and at home, they find the support they need for learning. But when social capital from these sources is not readily available, students generate it for themselves by turning more and more to the student subculture for support. One reason that young people willingly join gangs and willingly join less formal cliques is that gangs and cliques provide a form of social capital that substitutes for the forms of social capital schools and communities should be providing. But membership in neither is free. The price of belonging is to adopt the group's norms. The all too frequent result is the development of norms-based codes of behavior that work against what schools are trying to do.

Schools develop academic capital by becoming focused communities that cultivate a deep culture of teaching and learning. The rituals, norms, commitments, and traditions of this culture become the framework that motivates and supports student learning and development. In focused communities teaching and learning provide the basis for making important school decisions. Leaders in focused communities are committed to the principle that "form should follow function," with function being defined by school goals and purposes. In a focused community there is a strong and clear commitment to student achievement as evidenced by rigorous academic work, teachers' personal concern for student success, and the expectations that students will work hard (see, for example, Sebring and Bryk 1996).

Having an academic focus and providing a caring community for students are both important. But neither the caring needed nor the learning needed can be easily packaged, scripted, and imported. Both must emerge from the school's own sense of what is important, the school's own inventory of values and purposes, the school's own commitment to do well, and from other cultural concerns that provide a school with character.

What are the characteristics that help schools become focused and caring communities that contribute to student learning? In reviewing the research on capital development and school effectiveness, Hill and Celio identify the following: "small school size, personalization, high expectations for all students regardless of family background, teacher collaboration, aggressive leadership, simplicity of the curriculum, consistent standards for student behavior and effort, and family and peer group support" (1998: 30). These characteristics are related to building community in one form or another, a topic we explored in Chapter 4.

CAPITAL DEVELOPMENT AND SCHOOL EFFECTIVENESS

1 small school size;
2 high expectations for all students regardless of family background;
3 teacher collaboration;
4 aggressive leadership;
5 simplicity of the curriculum;
6 consistent standards for student behavior and effort;
7 family and peer group support.

In sum, schools which function as focused communities where unique values are important; schools where caring for each other is the norm; schools where academic matters count; and schools where social covenants are established that bring parents, teachers, students, and others together in a shared commitment to the common good are able to use the values of the lifeworld in their work and, as a result, do surprisingly well in enhancing student achievement. This link between the lifeworld of a school and that school's effectiveness establishes local authority as a necessary ingredient in any school effectiveness equation.

It is much easier to identify the lifeworld qualities that are common to effective schools than to develop a one-best list of characteristics. Effective schools often differ in the standards they pursue, the way they organize for teaching and learning, the curriculum they teach, and in the pedagogies they favor. Sara Lawrence Lightfoot documents these differences in her seminal book *The Good High School* (1983). She provides portraits of six very different, but still very good high schools. What emerged from her study was that a single list of indicators for a good school is not so easily identified. Good schools are unique and good schools are diverse. They serve different neighborhoods, contain different mixes of goals and purposes, use different ways to achieve these goals and purposes, and have heads who provide their own unique blend of leadership strategies and styles. Goodness builds and grows from what a particular school and its community value. The lifeworld of a school, not excessive externally imposed organizational structures or outside mandates, is what counts the most.

> *"Good schools are unique and good schools are diverse."*

Standards and standardization

It is difficult to create schools with character when states[1] seek to impose the same expectations and the same outcomes for learning across the curriculum on all schools. For this reason the present standards movement catching fire in many parts of the world may have some unanticipated negative consequences and may need rebalancing if we are to get the benefits of standards and protect the lifeworlds of schools at the same time.

Increasingly the standards movement seeks to identify a single set of standards and uses a standardized assessment system for all of the children in a given jurisdiction. Standardizing everything that will be learned and standardizing how these learnings will be assessed may not be a problem if the jurisdiction is a single school or a small school district. But when this jurisdiction is significantly larger, then we may have problems. Take the state of Texas in the USA, for example. Texas is geographically, economically, and culturally diverse. Its governor often speaks of the state as being the seventh largest economy in the world. The number of students enrolled in its 7,000 K-12 schools in 1999 was 3.9 million. The state has over 1,000 independent school districts. Having one set of standards and one state testing program to assess these standards assumes that virtually all of these students, schools, and communities have the same learning needs and interests and, therefore, all of the students in the state should be expected to learn the same thing. Further, no allowance is made for differences in the economic needs of different geographical regions of the state or in the wishes of local students and their local school boards regarding matters of standards, curriculum, and assessment. One set of standards is presumed to fit all.

This commitment to standardization places community building at risk and compromises the discretion that parents, teachers, students, and local communities need to decide for themselves what their goals and purposes should be, what values they should pursue, and what it is they want their schools to accomplish. One way to avoid this problem is by switching to layered standards that give both the state and local schools a share in the responsibility to set and assess standards. Another way to avoid this problem is by broadening the base of assessments.

Before we examine these themes in more detail, let's consider why present policies favor standardization. By taking the position that if you are going to have rigorous standards for learning they need to be the same for everyone, many states in the USA and throughout the world are confusing rigorous standards with standardization. The two are often thought to be the same. But it is possible, even desirable, to have rigorous standards that differ for different schools. For example, a high school that wants to specialize in the performing arts would be irresponsible if it did not prepare its students to demonstrate high levels of literacy in reading, writing, and other forms of communication, in basic math, and in civics. It would be equally irresponsible if this school did not place special emphasis on performing arts learning objectives and the academic disciplines that directly support these objectives. If this school were standards based, it might have some standards that would be the same as a neighboring school and lots of standards that would be different. Further, many of the standards that differ in this school would lend themselves better to performance-based assessments and to other kinds of data collection than to just standardized paper and pencil tests. Both forms of assessment should count in deciding whether this school meets its responsibilities to its publics.

Sometimes adopting uniform standards is viewed as a way to ensure equity. In the state of Florida, for example, each school is given a letter grade A, B, C, D, or F, depending upon how that school performs on the state's standards-based tests, on dropout rates, and on other indicators. About 80 percent of the schools given As and Bs reported that the percentage of students receiving free or reduced-priced lunch (a common measure of poverty in the USA) at school was below the state average of 43 percent. By contrast, 96 percent of the schools given Ds and Fs by the state were above average in the number of students receiving free or reduced lunch (Sandham 2000).

In the name of equity Florida's commissioner of education defends the state accountability system by arguing for the need to maintain a common standard. "We recognize that schools in low-income areas face challenges. But we're not going to have two standards – one for schools that face a lot of challenges, and one for schools that don't" (quoted in ibid.: 19). The executive director of the Florida School Boards Association thinks differently about the standards and equity issue. "Yes, all students can learn. But they start from different starting points and [state officials] have failed to take that into consideration" (quoted in ibid.: 19). Those who make the rules for competitive golf and horse racing, incidentally, feel the same way. Golfers are given handicaps based on their average scores over time and these handicaps are used to adjust their actual scores in a competitive match. Jockeys are weighed and weights are added to the saddles of lighter jockeys to compensate for any advantage they may have over heavier jockeys.

The other side of the standards and equity coin is how standards are assessed. Should the emphasis be on rating schools and states based on absolute standardized test scores? Or should the emphasis be on the value schools and states add to student levels of achievement? Consider the US states Arkansas and Maine as examples (see Barton 1999). The average scores for fourth graders on the 1992 National Assessment of Educational Progress (NAEP) math tests were 210 for Arkansas and 232 for Maine. The average scores for eighth graders on the 1996 NAEP math tests were 262 and 284. On an absolute level Maine students scored 22 points higher in 1996 than did Arkansas students. But in terms of student achievement gains from 1992 to 1996, Arkansas and Maine are in a statistical dead heat – each having gained 52 points. When comparing Arkansas and Maine on an absolute level, Maine wins. But when comparing the two in terms of value-added student learning over the four-year period, declaring a winner is not so easy. Most readers would probably give the edge to Arkansas, given their 1992 scores.

This difference in views among states and other stakeholders points to a major consideration when standards policy is made – standards are judgements, judgements are expressions of values, and values count. Judgements, however, differ. Different judgements lead to different standards. And that is why differentiated standards should be considered.

Advocating differentiated standards is not the same as advocating doing away with standards. Setting standards for what students need to know, for the levels of civility that should characterize student behavior, for how parents, teachers, and school-board members should define their roles, for teacher learning, and in other areas is a good thing for students, a good thing for schools, and a good thing for the state. The right standards and the right assessments can help members of a school and its community define the common good and to come together in a common quest to pursue that good. When this happens both standards and assessments play an important role in helping to build the kind of focused and caring communities that research tells us are most effective for our students.

But, as pointed out earlier, when only uniform standards are mandated for everyone in a state, they can erode local discretion, place the school's organizational character at risk, compromise its ability to be responsive to local needs and aspirations, and ultimately hamper its efforts to provide effective teaching and learning.

A further problem is one of representation. States are often criticized for being too top down in developing standards and in requiring the implementation of standards by local schools – a stance they often deny. They point out that parents, teachers, testing experts, politicians, and corporate leaders are typically represented on state-appointed committees that are charged with writing standards or with jurying standards.[2] But the vast majority of ordinary people do not have a direct role or a direct say in this process. Though democratic government in the form of representative participation by those elected or appointed may be the best way to handle most decisions that affect our lives, when issues have to do with our children, their social and mental health, their civic and intellectual development, and their spiritual and moral growth then democratic government in the form of direct participation of those affected by the issues at hand may be more appropriate than representative participation.

The state has an important role to play in this process and so do parents, teachers, students, and other citizens in local schools and in local communities. Sure, there are some things that everyone should learn, but there are also some things that might be learned by some students but not others; in one school but not another school; in one state but not another state. In setting standards for our schools the principle of subsidiarity should reign. This lifeworld friendly principle states that every member of a society should be free from unnecessary intervention, circumscription, and regulation by the state. When states have faith in the ability and moral capacity of those closest to the action to make good decisions, they show it by adopting the principle of subsidiarity. Subsidiarity is not just about democratic values, one's philosophy of life or view of human nature. It is about the bottom line, too. When corporations practice the principle of subsidiarity they make more money. When research enterprises practice the principle of subsidiarity they register more patents and solve more problems. And when educational systems practice the principle of subsidiarity, students learn more. In every case the reason is the same. Subsidiarity develops the capacity and will of people and makes enterprises more adaptive. The principle of subsidiarity, in other words, encourages and enables learning, commitment, and change.

> *"Every member of a society should be free from unnecessary intervention, circumscription, and regulation by the state."*

Are standards objective?

Standards can be intimidating. My dictionary defines a standard as something set up by an authority as a rule to measure the quality and quantity of something. Many ordinary citizens come to think of a learning standard or a school standard as something similar to the gold standard – a scientific and objective measure of something valuable that ordinary people had better not challenge. Thus, parents and other citizens rarely ask what a standards-based, state-assigned school rating such as A, B, C, D, F means. They just assume that whatever is being measured should be measured and whatever the ratings are they must be scientific ones. But, standards are neither objective nor scientific. They are subjective. Some standards are good and some are bad. Some standards are measured properly and some are not. In some cases the rating schemes designed to measure standards are set too high. And in other cases the rating schemes are set too low. There is no educational atomic clock that provides a sure meta standard against which other standards of measurement can be compared.

Keeping the standards record straight on the objectivity issue is an important responsibility of school leadership. Setting standards is a process best served by broad-based, reasoned consideration and deliberate action – neither of which are possible when parents and other citizens are "moon-struck" by images of standards as infallible and unchallengeable. If there are three things we need to converse with government officials, parents, and other citizens about, it is that standards are statements of values, values, and values. Our message should be: standards are set by people who make human decisions about what they believe or think is appropriate or is not appropriate. Not surprisingly these people often differ. One group, for example, might prefer some standards, accept others, and reject still others, while another group in the same room dealing with the same standards might prefer, accept, or reject different ones. We have little to gain by viewing the setting of standards across the curriculum as a zero-sum game where some people win and others lose. By not considering standards and standardization as the same thing, our eyes are opened to other alternatives.

Many readers assume that standard setting may be values based in some areas, but is certainly objective in the hard sciences such as mathematics or science or the basic skill areas such as reading. After all, $2 + 2 = 4$; H_2O is water; and cat is spelled C-A-T. But the evidence indicates otherwise. In California the setting of science standards by a state-appointed committee turned out to be a difficult task. The committee splintered into two groups: one group favored an inquiry approach and the other group favored a content-acquisition approach.

The first group pushed for standards that would help students think like scientists, experience science first hand, learn general scientific principles, and be able to solve scientific problems. The second group pushed for standards that were more graded and content oriented. In the end the committee members reached a compromise. The California State Board of Education refused to accept the compromise package, deciding instead to approve the second group's version of science standards (Olson 1998; and Hoff 1998).

What about in the skill areas such as reading? Is setting standards in this area controversial too? In 1993 the US Department of Education commissioned the National Council of Teachers of English, the International Reading Association, and the Center for the Study of Reading at the University of Illinois, Urbana, to develop and recommend a set of national standards in reading. When the standards were submitted, the Department, not liking them, rejected the work and terminated funding of the project (Clinchy 1995). Later they appointed another committee and subsequently accepted their work.

Here is another example. By law, the state of Texas requires that most of the words in first grade reading textbooks be phonics based or decodable. In the past the Texas Educational Agency (charged with implementing state policies) has interpreted "most" to mean 51 percent of the words. Recently, the Texas State Board of Education, which oversees the agency, ordered the agency to raise the percentage of decodable words to 80 percent. Different percentages of decodable words mean different reading standards will be set. Though one could argue that there is evidence justifying increasing the percentage of words to 80 percent, there is ample evidence pointing in the other direction as well. The issue of phonics is about more than what research says – it's about values.

Imagine passing laws and other regulations that require physicians to prescribe aspirin (i.e. Bayer) over acetaminophen (Tylenol) at least 80 percent of the time. It just wouldn't happen and it shouldn't happen in education either. Yet, even in the basic skills areas such as reading, different ideologies lead to different conclusions. Standards setting in the real world resembles a game of winning and

"If you want standards that you like, make sure the people who set the standards are people you agree with."

losing rather than a process of scientific inquiry into a discipline in search of some sort of truth. Simply put, standards are subjective reflections of those who set them. Different people set different standards. Thus, the process is as much political as it is anything else. If you want standards that you like, make sure the people who set the standards are people you agree with.

Preserving the lifeworld

Subjectivity shouldn't scare us. In a democracy politics should play an important role in setting standards and in other matters. But the schooling of one's children and other lifeworld concerns are so important that *hardball* win/lose approaches to deciding which standards to choose should be avoided. It should not be a matter of all or none. When 60 percent of the people prefer one set of standards and 40 percent the other, instead of forcing everyone to accept the standards of the majority we should consider legitimizing two different sets of standards. One way that more people can win is by having differentiated standards. With different standards, some would be common for all but most would be diverse. Some would be decided centrally, but most would be decided locally.

With the right policies in place standards have both the potential to provide schools and communities with the needed focus and the potential to rally the human resources of a school and school district in a common direction. And with the right policies in place, testing can be a powerful tool to help assess how well standards are being achieved. Both can help schools get better. If standards and testing per se are not the issue, what is? The issue is the erosion of the lifeworld of schools and local communities. Under present policies, instead of standards and accountability being derived from the needs, purposes, and interests of parents, teachers, and students in each school and each community, the standards and accountability systems are determining what are these needs and purposes and interests. This is why I believe we need a system of accountability that is more responsive to local passions, needs, and values. We need a system of accountability where standards remain rigorous and trustworthy, but are not presumed to be standardized. We need a system of accountability where tests and other assessments possess the proper psychometric properties and have substance of integrity, while still allowing the specifics of what is tested to reflect local values and preferences.

A layered approach to standards

We can create a lifeworld-responsive system of rigorous and trustworthy accountability that includes testing and other assessments and that includes public disclosure of results if we are willing to adopt a layered approach to standards and a shared approach to accountability with a strong local component. Moving in this direction will mean rethinking the one-best way we do things in schools. Moving in this direction will mean forging a new partnership that brings together the state, local school districts, and individual schools in search of the common good. Moving in this direction will require that schools be viewed as communities of responsibility as discussed in Chapter 4. Communities of responsibility make known what their purposes are, make promises to the public as to what they hope to accomplish, engage in rigorous inquiry to ensure that promises are kept, and *invite public scrutiny of their intents, actions, and results*. Before moving on to what a system of layered standards and assessments might look like, let's summarize with some assertions:

SETTING STANDARDS

- States should participate in setting standards for schools.
- School boards, parents, and teachers at the local school and even students should also participate in setting standards.
- When standards and assessments are set by the state alone, standardization is likely to emerge with schools becoming more and more similar as a result.
- When school boards, parents, teachers, and students at the local level participate in the setting of standards and in determining assessments, schools become standardized in some few areas but diverse in most others.
- Letting parents choose the schools their children will attend only has meaning when students, parents, and teachers are provided with real options to choose from.

- The state should assume responsibility for developing standards and assessments for all schools in the areas of reading, writing, math, and civics.
- Citizens, parents, teachers, and students at the local level should share in the responsibility for developing standards and assessments in all other areas of the curriculum.
- Since school districts and schools within them differ, it should be expected that many standards will differ as one moves from district to district and from school to school within the same district.
- The state has a responsibility to provide both technical assistance and professional development for helping schools set standards and develop assessments.
- The state has a responsibility to provide a centralized standards bank from which local authorities might draw as needed.
- Students should participate by setting standards for themselves and by assessing their own performance.
- Student assessments should count along with state, school district, and local school assessments in evaluating a school.
- The state should provide constructive oversight by ensuring that the standards set locally and the assessments developed locally are defensible and trustworthy. Developing standards for standards and standards for assessments would help.
- No single set of standards and no single assessment system should dominate the other (adapted from Sergiovanni 2000: 89–91).

The language of accountability

We don't think about it much, but the language we use shapes the way we see things, what we believe, and how we behave. That is why I think leaders need to pay attention to the language of accountability and should strive to create a new language more open and responsive to local needs and aspirations. Part of the language of accountability is the concept of rigor. We need, we are told, rigorous standards for what students must know and we need rigorous tests to ensure that students reach these standards. As a word, rigor has its appeal. Those who advocate rigor, for example, make it clear in no uncertain terms that they are tough cookies. This ring of rhetoric typically wins points for those who speak it. But I worry that too much emphasis on rigor may lead to educational rigor mortis. According to *Webster's Seventh Collegiate Dictionary* rigor means *harsh, inflexibility in opinion, temper, or judgement; SEVERITY; the quality of being unyielding or inflexible; STRICTNESS; AUSTERITY; a condition that makes life difficult, challenging, or uncomfortable; strict precision; EXACTNESS.* When these ideas are unyieldingly applied to children in our K-12 schools, the result, too often, is rigor mortis – defined as *temporary rigidity of muscles after death.*

Sure, standards ought to be high and, sure, students should to be challenged in ways consistent with their developmental levels. But being responsive to these levels requires a certain flexibility that exclusive attention to rigor cannot allow. Too often the rhetoric of rigor leads to policies that are not sensible stretches for children, but arbitrary obstacles that can have lifelong negative consequences. Insisting that a student with an above average academic record (except in math) and who has twice failed the state graduation examination in math with scores of 69 and 67 (70 needed to pass) be denied a diploma, and thus be denied access to the Marine Corps or access to a job at the local lumber yard (at the state's urging, the company's policy is to hire only high school graduates) is an example.

We can do better than rigorous. What about authentic? Authentic means *AUTHORITATIVE; worthy of acceptance or belief; trustworthy; not imaginary, false or imitation; genuine.* Authentic doesn't quite communicate toughness the way rigor does, but it does communicate a certain solidness. Authentic standards are solid standards that you can trust will help students and teachers do better and are worthy of your acceptance. Solid standards are tough in a developmentally honest way or they wouldn't be trustworthy. But tough standards are not always solid. The language of rigor will probably not go away. But maybe we can communicate its

> *"How do we determine if student learning is rigorous and authentic?"*

virtues while taking off its sharp edges of rigidity by using the terms rigorous and authentic together as in "rigorous and authentic standards and assessments."

Standards for intellectual work

How do we determine if student learning is rigorous and authentic? How do we find out if schools are making intellectual demands of students that respect high quality? How do we determine if students are rising to these demands? So far, in the USA, the UK, and many other countries we pretty much rely on the results of standardized basic skills tests. Such tests help but are not enough. Newmann, Lopez and Bryk point out that test scores give a partial picture of what students know and can do. "The standardized test score gives a numerical indicator of how a student performed relative to other students, but does not show the specific knowledge or skills the student demonstrated (or failed to demonstrate)" (1998: 7). Further, while conventional work may be important and thus assessed, rigorous and authentic student work goes beyond, representing more complex accomplishments. As Newmann, Lopez and Bryk point out: "'Authentic' is used here not to suggest that conventional work by students is unimportant to them and their teachers, or that basic skills and proficiencies are to be devalued, but only to identify some kinds of intellectual work as more complex and socially or personally meaningful than others" (ibid.: 12). To them authentic intellectual work "involves original application of knowledge and skills (rather than just routine use of facts and procedures). It also entails disciplined inquiry into the details of a particular problem, and results in a product or presentation that has meaning or value beyond success in school" (p. 12). They refer to these criteria as construction of knowledge; through disciplined inquiry; to produce learning that has value beyond school.

In the real world of work, competent adults routinely construct knowledge because the problems they face cannot be solved by simply using information and skills previously learned. Unquestionably the basics are important, but they are not enough. Competence, in our complex world, requires using what we know to *construct new knowledge* that is relevant to the problem being faced.

But, as Newmann and his colleagues point out, constructing solutions to problems doesn't mean that anything goes. This construction must be accompanied by *disciplined inquiry*, meaning knowing how to use a prior-knowledge base that includes frameworks, theories, algorithms, and other conventions. The basics are, of course, an important part of this prior-knowledge base. Further, the use of disciplined inquiry should reflect in-depth understanding of the problem. And finally, the use of disciplined inquiry involves the ability to use complex verbal, symbolic, and visual modes of communication. "If students are to achieve authentic intellectual accomplishments, they must learn to communicate in more elaborate forms" (ibid.: 14). For knowledge to be authentic, claim Newmann and his colleagues, it must have value in some utilitarian, aesthetic, or personal way, beyond simply confirming that a school objective has been met. Quizzes, exams, spelling bees may have their place but the proof of authentic learning is in its relationship to real-world problems and issues; in the ability of students to understand them, to engage them, and to offer defensible solutions.

Rigorous and authentic learning is best assessed by collecting direct evidence of the intellectual work students do. Observing and rating student performances, as done in the arts through exhibitions and recitals, or as done in physical education through field days, would be ideal. But there are many other ways to assess the intellectual quality of teaching and learning that are more efficient. Newmann and Wehlage (1995) and Newmann, Secada and Wehlage (1995) propose, for example, collecting samples of the assignments that teachers give and collecting samples of the actual work that students do. Focusing on writing and math, the Newmann researchers have developed standards for assignments given and standards for student work done along with protocols for assessing these standards. The assignments indicate the intellectual demands teachers make and the students' work indicates levels of mastery they address in the areas of constructing knowledge, disciplined inquiry, and value beyond school. The protocols were used recently to assess the quality of intellectual work in Chicago's schools (see Newmann, Lopez and Bryk 1998).

The standards for intellectual work discussed above have a number of virtues. Instead of mandating all of the standards that a school must teach and instead of relying on uniform testing programs to assess the extent to which teachers are meeting these standards, the standards for intellectual work approach lets teachers and students set standards for themselves. Further, this approach provides a rigorous and authentic way of assessing the suitability of these standards. The standards provided are, in essence, standards for standards. Though many standards exist, only some meet this criterion. In a layered system, where many standards will differ as one moves from school to school, the question of whether a given school's standards have integrity or not is an important one. And finally, the extent to which teachers are actually teaching to rigorous and authentic standards and the extent to which student learning reflects these rigorous and authentic standards are also assessed.

The standards for intellectual work process are both summative and formative. They can tell a school and the state what students are learning and at what level students are learning. They can also tell what teachers are teaching and what levels of quality this teaching is addressing. If rigor and authenticity are rare as student work is assessed, clues as to why this might be could be found in the assignments that teachers provide students. Patterns across many samples of student work can reveal if a learning problem is systemic (caused perhaps by poor design of the curriculum, the need for more teacher development, or other reasons) or targeted (Johnny has difficulty in grasping a particular kind of concept or in using certain basic skills).

Some tentative proposals

In developing a system of layered standards I propose that there be standards in five areas:

- Uniform standards for all schools in basic reading, writing, and math (maybe civics).
- Varied standards in key curriculum areas such as history, advanced math, English, art, music, social science.
- Varied standards in social and emotional learning areas including character development.
- School standards in non-curriculum areas such as teacher development, use of resources, and sense of community.
- Teacher standards in such areas as professionalism, collegiality, and professional growth.

The state might assume responsibility for setting the uniform standards in the basic skills areas. These areas would be assessed by standardized tests. For the varied standards in the key curriculum areas, the states might assume some of the responsibility but the local school and local community would assume most of the responsibility. For the varied standards in social and emotional learning, the state and local authorities might share equally in setting standards. For school standards in non-curriculum areas, the state and local authorities might develop standards together. With respect to teachers' standards, the state might assume major responsibility with active participation by the local school and community. If the state sets up an independent professional teaching board to oversee teaching standards, then the distribution would be different with the board playing the major role.

Though standardized tests would dominate in assessing uniform standards in basic reading, math, and writing (and perhaps civics), they would play a much less important role for the varied standards in key curriculum areas, a negligible role in assessing the varied standards in social and emotional areas, and no role in assessing school standards and teacher standards. In these areas the dominant assessment vehicle would be a whole school quality review process (see, for example, Ancess 1996; Bryk et al. 1998; and Sergiovanni 2000). This process would involve both an internal self-study conducted by the school and its community and an external study conducted by an external visitation team (the whole school quality review team) that would engage in an intensive examination of each individual school.

> External reviews should begin in the classroom with the actual quality of student work, and then move from there to consider the schools' overall development efforts. To guide such analysis, the external reviews must be grounded both in standards for student learning [see, for example, Newmann's work discussed earlier] and a larger framework of effective school organization and development.
>
> (Bryk et al. 1998: 300)

Visits might take place every four years.

In the social and emotional areas performance exhibitions, portfolios, and perhaps a service requirement would make sense. For school standards in non-curriculum areas it might make sense for the state to develop some sort of indicator system that the whole school quality review team would have to consider along with local self-study data. A similar approach might work for teachers' standards if no independent teachers' standards board exists in the state. Making decisions about who would be responsible for what requires a great deal of deliberation by everyone. But to get the conversation started I would suggest the state be responsible for assessing standards in basic reading, math, and writing. Its findings would have to be considered by the whole school quality review team as it brings together information from a variety of sources to reach conclusions about the school. The whole school quality review team would be the major player in all other assessments. This team would develop one report that provides an in-depth study of the school and a summary rating that takes into account all layers of standards and their assessments. No one source of data would be used alone in reaching a summative evaluation. In order of importance the audience for the report would be the local school, the local school community, the school district, the state, and the general public.

Combining localism with public disclosure

Though local in origin the school quality review process would have to be opened widely to the public. Beginning with a self-study that inventories the promises a given school is making to its local community, its students, its teachers, and to itself, the school would then detail how it expects to keep those promises and the evidence it is providing for having kept those promises. An external review team, comprised of teachers, administrators, board members, business people, and other citizens from a disinterested neighboring community (as well as state officials) would then visit the school for a period of several days. External reviews would be grounded in the school's promises and school improvement plans, in some minimum requirements set by the state, as well as widely accepted standards for teaching and learning, teacher development, and school effectiveness.

One virtue of a school quality review process is that over time (say a school is thoroughly reviewed every four years) baseline data can be established and used to judge progress. This value-added feature is a virtue not found in the more hurried, one-shot testing programs that now characterize accountability systems across the globe. The review team would have to take into account student results on state-required tests in the basic skills of math, reading, writing, and perhaps civics in its write-up. The write-up should be distributed widely at the local level, to the state, perhaps even summarized and published in the local newspaper, and made available in its entirety on the internet. This sort of public disclosure has its disadvantages as well as advantages. But I believe a good accountability system is based on trust. A system that is locally oriented must be viewed as trustworthy by local citizens, the state, and other legitimate interests. One way to earn trust is through public disclosure. Thus, my vote, at the moment, would be for full and wide disclosure of the report.

School visitations are not a new idea. Most, however, bring with them detailed frameworks in the form of lists of standards that the schools being visited must provide evidence they are meeting. If the school quality review process evolves in this direction, then it probably will not work. What is needed is a system that is local in origin, that is anchored in some overarching conceptualization, but that allows the majority of standards to be generated by the local community. Further, though it is likely to be a challenge, emphasis needs to be placed on the real thing rather than on the accumulation of paperwork. Thus, visiting teams would spend a good deal of their time interviewing students, teachers, parents, and others, shadowing students, examining student work, visiting classrooms, and paying particular attention to the sorts of standards for quality intellectual work suggested by Newmann and his colleagues earlier in this chapter.

Leadership and the lifeworld

Perhaps the most basic of leadership principles is that a school becomes and stays effective by building on its lifeworld. In school leadership it is the theory, not the specifics, that count. This idea was central to Sara Lightfoot's findings about commonalties among "good" schools discussed earlier. And it is central to Teske and Schneider's (1999) recent research on characteristics of successful schools in New York City. While the researchers were able to conclude that these schools were blessed with strong and consistent head leadership, how this leadership was provided and the school cultures that this leadership created were very different. In their words:

> Each principal [head] we studied was integral to defining the culture of the school, whether they had created it or adapted to it. At the elementary school level, Kurz's exceptional professionalism and organizational skills coupled with a quiet but stern demeanor

structure the atmosphere of the school: Students walked in orderly lines, teachers dressed in professional business attire, and attention was paid to the cleanliness of the school. Kase's approach employed similar characteristics, but in a more relaxed environment. At the other extreme, Foster's open approach to child development and problem solving is mirrored by her collective office space; students, parents, teachers, and even a rabbit frequent Foster's space, a spatial exemplar of the constant interaction between students, staff, and administration. In between, Carmichael simultaneously fashioned a sense of leadership, respect, and authority for herself, while stressing the importance of teachers' contributions and collaboration.

(ibid.: 21)

Despite these differences, Teske and Schneider found that each of these exceptional heads worked to develop a clear and focused school culture, and a community that supported that culture. They had a strong set of values and worked to develop a coherent mission and vision for their schools. Clearly, not anything goes. Some educational decisions are better than others. Further, absolute relativism in the long run leads to a vacuous leadership practice which will likely take its toll on a school's effectiveness. But the point remains, it is the theory that is more important than the specifics.

Larry Cuban (1998) argues that successful schools come in many different shapes and styles. Some are traditional. Others are progressive. And others are somewhere in the middle. But regardless of their form, successful schools share three characteristics: parents, teachers, and students are satisfied with them; they are successful in achieving their own goals and objectives; and their graduates exhibit democratic values, attitudes, and behaviors. This unique focus and the support that parents, teachers, and students give it are key. To use the language of this chapter, successful schools have character. In the descriptions above, local passions, local beliefs, local participation, and local support are key to school effectiveness. We are not likely to get very far in cultivating these virtues of localism unless we rethink our present course in developing standards and assessments. This rethinking, I believe, will be key to the future of school leadership.

QUESTIONS FOR FURTHER EXPLORATION

1   What do you understand by "rigor"? What do you think is
    understood by that term:
    by politicians?
    by headteachers?
    by parents?
    by school governors?

2   Fourteen principles for setting standards are given in this
    chapter. Look through them considering your endorsement
    for each of these from strong to weak. You may also go
    through them considering how each of these is reflected in
    practice in your own school.

3   A useful professional development activity would be to draw
    up a writing scale on the following pattern:

proactive in own school		important
1		
2		
1 2 3 4	3	1 2 3 4
agree disagree	4	low high
5		
6		
7		
8		
9		
10		
11		
12		
13		
14		

6 Leadership and learning

Searching for a practical theory

Look, I know I am supposed to respond to student needs and interests and staying with this unit on Macbeth one more week would have lots of learning benefits. But I have a curriculum to cover if the kids are going to be ready for the state's proficiency exam. Ready or not, we have to move on.

Sure, I know that delegating responsibility and involving staff usually lead to better decisions. But on this one, the decision has to be A or I am in trouble. I can't take the risk that involving staff might lead to their choosing B instead. Then what would I do?

Barbara divided her school into three houses in order to get the scale down and it worked for her. My school is the same size. When I tried to downscale, I did everything she did. And I did it in the same way. But in my case it turned out to be a disaster. Is there nothing that works for sure?

I used the same checklist of competencies to evaluate all the heads in the district. Even though they get similar scores by displaying the same leadership behaviors in the same way, some are more effective than others. Roland Barth (1990) suggests the same behaviors displayed in different contexts get different results. If he is right, how can anyone know what to do?

These anecdotes may lead you to wonder both whether leadership and whether teaching can ever evolve into disciplined fields of inquiry and practice. I think they can – but, as this book argues, not unless we understand the differences between being rational and being rationalistic. When a head is behaving rationally, her or his behavior relies on reason that takes into account specific contexts and that recognizes different contexts lead to different perceptions and realities. What makes sense is a mixture of knowledge that is absolute and knowledge that is constructed by contexts. When a head is behaving in a rationalistic way her or his behavior relies on reason that is independent of context and which is superior to sense perception. Contexts are not very important. Sense perception does not count very much. What makes sense is singular and absolute – applying to all situations in the same way.

Let's examine these differences within leadership. A rational discipline of leadership gives more emphasis to developing strategies that reflect a higher concern for values than for discreet goals, for patterns of learning and patterns of behavior than for discreet outcomes, for learning how to ride the wave rather than for plowing straight ahead (Sergiovanni 1987). Leaders work with multiple goals and with ill-defined, ever-changing contexts. Their style of inquiry and practice resembles surfing more than linear thinking. In a rational discipline of learning good decisions are important. A good decision reflects what we believe is right for schools and what we believe is in concert with our values as a school community. Sometimes good decisions are not very effective in the sense that they cost more, are inconvenient to implement, or are difficult to evaluate. Ideally, good decisions are effective ones too. For this reason, in a rational discipline of leadership *accuracy* is the first priority. Leaders struggle to understand contexts, make decisions, and pursue solutions regardless of the difficulty they experience in trying to nail this accuracy down. *Precision*, though valued and pursued rigorously, is secondary.

How carefully we measure our purposes and standards, for example, is a precision problem. How meaningful are our purposes and standards is an accuracy problem. Accuracy should not be sacrificed to convenience, nor should important questions be sacrificed to trivial ones simply because the trivial ones are easier to answer. The cardinal rule, in a rational discipline of leadership, is that something not worth doing is not worth doing well. Emphasizing precision over accuracy is like the person who lost her keys in the middle of the block, but looked for them at the street corner because the light was better. We do this, for example, when we adopt simple tests because they are easier to score and when we forgo more complex evaluation strategies such as portfolios, performance exhibitions, and internships because they are difficult to score.

Andy Hargreaves and Michael Fullan argue the case this way:

> Even when you know what research and published advice tells you, no one can prescribe exactly how to apply what you have learned to your particular school and all the unique problems, opportunities and peculiarities it contains. Your own organization has its own special combination of personalities and prehistories. There is no one answer to the question of how one brings about change in specific situations. You can get ideas, directions, insights, and lines of thought, but you can never know exactly how to proceed. You have to beat the path by walking it.
>
> Today's leaders must learn to think through solutions themselves (with assistance from their colleagues and communities). This is the essence of the learning organization. Management ideas and techniques are helpful, but only in the service of a critical mindset where educators draw deeply on their own local knowledge and insights.
>
> (1998: 27)

One way to navigate through such complex questions is by viewing schools as being more like "complex adaptive systems" (Waldrop cited in Freedman 1992) than clockwork bureaucracies that run like well-oiled machines or organic bureaucracies that run like professionally organized decision-making hierarchies with bounded autonomy to ensure that the "right" decisions get made. (Setting the ends to be met but delegating the means to achieve them is an example of bounded autonomy.)

Complex adaptive systems include the ecology of lakes, colonies of bees, and the human brain. These systems, according to Freedman (1992) and according to the world-famous complexity researchers at the Santa Fe Institute who study them, share several characteristics. They are *self-managing* in the sense that the systems consist of webs or networks of "agents" or "components" that act independently of each other without guidance from any form of central authority or control. Yet these same independent agents or components are able to engage in *cooperative behavior* or in reciprocal interactions which resemble living communities that function at a higher level than any agent or component could alone. In schools this work in unison is more than a collection of "I"s. It is, instead, the coming together into a We. How can that be? How can, for example, people in schools function as and be part of a community when they may not physically work together and when coordination among them is implicit rather than explicit?

Using analogies from the natural world can help answer these complex questions. Take, for example, how honeybees solve the problem of finding the best food sources available and of getting the most out of these sources (this account by Morse 1992 is drawn from Sergiovanni 1996: 41–3). Their success depends upon the behavior of individual bees who make their own independent decisions rather than on a hierarchical structure within the colony, the specification of bee production quotas, or on bees working collaboratively to make shared decisions about where to hunt. Bees seem to practice a form of self-management. They function as a group of independent operators. Each bee makes her own decisions about which flower patches to work. Then each assesses the richness of the nectar source and engages in a dance that communicates to others whether this level of richness is low or high. Freedman notes that:

> A particular kind of feedback makes self-management possible. In a sense, self-organizing systems are learning systems but of a specific sort. Capable of "learning" through feedback from the external environment, they also "embed" that learning in their actual structure . . . In this way, self-organizing systems constantly rearrange themselves as the effects of previous actions or changes in external conditions ripple through the system. Information is embedded in the structure. As external conditions change, the structure of the system automatically changes.
>
> (1992: 32)

Bees are not picky about who is doing the dancing, but only about what the message is. Thus experienced bees are treated the same as bees with little or no experience. As Morse (1992) explains:

> What is now understood is that this is sufficient to direct the actions of the whole colony. A bee being recruited follows one dancer, and takes the advice of this bee, and forages accordingly. She then makes her own decision as to the profitability of the food source,

and may dance herself, or not, and continue to forage at the site, or not, depending upon what she thinks. The bees that dance longer are more likely to be encountered, and to recruit more bees. In this way the greatest number of bees get the best advice and forage at the best site.

(as cited in Sergiovanni 1996: 41–2)

The message that appeals to those who seek to apply complex adaptive systems thinking to schools is that the hive achieves order from the action of many independent bees. Bees are self-managing, and together comprise a network of individual actors that act independently and yet in unison, without guidance from any central source. They are not a mere collection of individuals who happen to be working in what appears to be interdependent ways. Instead, they are tied together into a colony of individual actors engaged in common purposes. Of course, there are limits in carrying these analogies too far. Bees, after all, are influenced by instinct and unusual forms of communication that may be genetically determined. These biological factors may, in fact, account for much of bee behavior. Still, it is clear that bees and other complex adaptive systems do not follow predetermined plans. They engage in a self-organizing process under conditions where management controls are impossible. And it is clear that this image provides a useful way to think about developing structures and leadership strategies for schools.

The leadership challenge for us is one of connections. How do we get students, teachers, parents, heads, and others connected to each other in authentic and meaningful ways under conditions that resemble complex adaptive systems? How can people become tied together and become tied to their work not just interpersonally, but morally and spiritually as well? The answer suggested in this book is to share a common moral quest, to be bonded to a set of shared conceptions, purposes, ideas, and values. What makes human systems unique is that they are not driven by just biological and psychological forces, but cultural forces as well. Cultural forces can help us find the balance needed to manage successfully in a complex world. Cultural forces rely on common purposes, values, commitments, and norms that result in relationships among people that have moral overtones; relationships that ensure caring and inclusiveness.

Controlling events or controlling probabilities?

Learning to lead differently in today's messy world of schooling is a little like asking teachers and heads to lead in uncharted waters. We just do not have a very good picture of what works in schools that resemble complex adaptive systems. Until we get a better picture we will have to struggle with some important questions:

TWO KEY QUESTIONS

* What lessons can be learned by using the complex adaptive systems metaphor as a model for organizing and leading schools?
* What changes will be needed in the ways that policy makers and school administrators seek to coordinate and direct the work of teachers and others toward desired ends?

The most important lesson may be to shift leadership from focusing on controlling events to focusing on controlling probabilities.

Theories of leadership are in the end theories of control. How do we increase the likelihood that good things will happen in a school – that our ends will be achieved? How do we ensure that all of the parts of the school will work together – that each member of the school will do the things that need to be done for us to be successful? How will we ensure that everyone will keep on learning so that their performance continuously improves? How do we ensure that motivation and commitment will be maintained – even increased? Control is intended to reduce ambiguity and indeterminacy, thus increasing reliability and predictability. But getting control is not as easy as it seems.

In seeking to control events rather than probabilities, policy makers throughout much of the world view the complex adaptive systems characteristic of schools as an evil that must be overcome in favor of order, reliability, and predictability. Thus, instead of accommodating to variation, the policies they develop seek to force schools into a mold of conformity. In an age of rapid change, of uncommon diversity, and of unprecedented complexity this strategy seems shortsighted.

Controlling events has many costs – some of which were discussed in the last chapter. Standards and outcomes thought to be important at time 1, for example, may be found less important at time 2. Standards not set and not assessed by state authorities are likely to be de-emphasized or excluded. By pursuing standards list A we do not pursue standards list B, even though the latter list may be more important for a large number of students, their parents, and communities.

Controlling probabilities

Controlling probabilities rather than events may make more sense. Probabilities are guided by strong values linked to purposes that provide direction. Specific standards and outcomes are still considered to be helpful but they emerge as schooling unfolds, as teaching takes place, and as a host of accompanying decisions by teachers and students are made. Like the bees discussed earlier, this emergence of strategies and outcomes *in use* allows schools to be responsive to the varied learning needs and interests they encounter.

With probabilities as the focus, schools are held accountable for ensuring that whatever specific outcomes are set at a given time and for a given group of standards – the probabilities are strong that they will reflect the school's values and contribute to the achievement of its purposes. Controlling events emphasizes seeking power over people and what they do. Controlling probabilities emphasizes using power to ensure that the likelihood of achieving values and purposes is increased. Often, increasing probabilities of success means giving up control over people and events – an idea found difficult to accept by many policy makers and school leaders.

Control strategies

What are our options when seeking control? Which of these options emphasize controlling events and which emphasize controlling probabilities? Following the work of Mintzberg (1979) it is useful to think of teachers, heads, and other leaders as having access to six strategies for ensuring control: direct supervision; standardizing the work that people do; standardizing the outcomes that must be achieved; standardizing the dispositions, knowledge, and skill that people must use to practice;

emphasizing common purposes and commitments; and emphasizing mutual adjustment as people work in teams or communities of practice.

No one control strategy is, in an absolute sense, better than another. The choice of strategy depends upon the extent to which it matches the nature of the work to be done, who is doing the work, the complexity of the work setting, and the standards of quality expected when work is completed. Where work complexity is simple, direct supervision involving telling people what to do, watching them do it, and making corrections as needed might be an appropriate choice. But as complexity increases, strategies closer to mutual adjustment make more sense.

Direct supervision, standardizing work processes, and even standardizing outcomes are usually appropriate and effective for simple work, but not for more complex work. These control strategies may well be the choices for the factory and the fast-food restaurant, but not for medical teams, high-tech companies, schools, and other enterprises where variation is important. In the former group controlling, scripting, and directing what it is that people do fit. There is no doubt about the outcomes to be achieved, the standards that should be used to judge outcomes, and the means by which one measures those standards. A Big Mac, for example, is designed to be exactly like every other Big Mac in every restaurant throughout the world. The standard of quality is the same as well. Each is cooked to exactly the same temperature and so on.

For schools and other enterprises that resemble complex adaptive systems obligating, professionalizing, and networking seem to be more appropriate as management options. These enterprises need to rely on purposing and shared values, standardizing knowledge and skills, and mutual adjustment as control strategies if they want to be successful. The reasons for their use are practical ones. The loose connectedness of complex adaptive systems does not make it easy to directly supervise what people are doing. Further, standardizing the work and standardizing outcomes too often result in work simplification, loss of meaning and significance, less satisfaction, and ultimately in poorer quality outcomes.

Mutual adjustment

Increasingly, standardizing knowledge and skills aimed at increasing the capacity of teachers to function more effectively is being used as a school improvement strategy. Further, relying on purposes and shared values has been recommended for providing the glue that brings people together in a loosely connected world. Less attention, however, has been given to mutual adjustment as a control strategy. To Mintzberg mutual adjustment involves the simple process of informal communications. For mutual adjustment to work, control of the work has to rest in the hands of the doers. Mintzberg argues that mutual adjustment is found naturally in the very simplest of organizations (he uses the example of two people in a canoe) and in the most complicated organizations. In his words:

> *"For mutual adjustment to work, control of the work has to rest in the hands of the doers."*

> Paradoxically, it is also used in the most complicated, because, as we shall see later, it is the only one that works under extremely difficult circumstances. Consider the organization charged with putting a man on the moon for the first time. Such an activity requires an incredibly elaborate division of labor, with thousands of specialists doing all kinds of specific jobs. But at the outset, no one can be sure exactly what needs to be done. That knowledge develops as the work unfolds. So in the final analysis, despite the use of other coordinating mechanisms, the success of the undertaking depends primarily on the ability of the specialists to adapt to each other along their uncharted route, not altogether unlike the two people in the canoe.
>
> (1979: 3)

The bees discussed earlier would no doubt feel comfortable with Mintzberg's description. He notes further:

> When the tasks are simple and routine, the organization is tempted to rely on the standardization of the work processes themselves. But more complex work may preclude this, forcing the organization to turn to the standardization of the outputs – specifying the results of the work but leaving the choice of process to the worker. In complex work, however, the outputs often cannot be standardized either, and so the organization must settle for standardizing the skills of the worker, if possible.

But should the divided tasks of the organization prove impossible to standardize, it may be forced to return full cycle, to favor the simplest, yet most adaptable coordinating mechanism – mutual adjustment . . . Sophisticated problem solvers facing extremely complicated situations must communicate informally if they are to accomplish their work.

(ibid.: 8)

The challenge, of course, is to figure out how to organize mutual adjustment in a way that makes sense in schools. Most schools have been working on the problem of teacher isolation and see the value of encouraging more teamwork among teachers. They started with an emphasis on congeniality. How do we improve the interpersonal climate in the schools so that teachers trust each other more, are more satisfied with their interpersonal relationships, and work together in greater harmony? Then they raised the stakes by moving beyond congeniality to collegiality. Collegiality is less concerned with interpersonal themes and more concerned with norms and values that define the faculty as a community of like-minded people connected together in a common commitment. Colleagues share common work traditions and help each other. Roland Barth points out that there are risks involved when teachers are engaged in observation, communication, sharing knowledge, and talking openly about their work. In his words:

Collegiality requires that everyone be willing to give up something without knowing in advance just what that may be. But the risks and costs of interdependence are nothing next to the risks and costs of sustaining a climate of emotional toxicity, of working in isolation, in opposite corners of the sandbox.

(1990: 32)

Mutual adjustment as a control strategy raises the stakes again as we move from an emphasis on collegiality alone to an emphasis on developing communities of practice. In communities of practice groups of teachers come to see themselves as being involved in a shared practice of teaching that transcends their own individual practices. Thus, they have an important stake not only in their own learning, but the learning of their colleagues. They are, as Stewart notes, "the shop floor of the human capital, the place where the stuff gets made" (1997: 96). Teachers function as communities of practice when they share a common body of knowledge, when they work together to expand that knowledge and to use it more effectively. Learning is key.

The importance of opportunity and capacity

At the center of leadership in today's schools, whether expressed by heads, teachers, or someone else, is organizational learning. This assertion is based on the simple but profound idea that if we expect schools to get continuously better at providing learning for students, teachers must become members of communities of practice and schools must become learning communities for adults as well as students. In Seymour Sarason's words: "It is virtually impossible to create and sustain over time conditions for productive learning for students when they do not exist for teachers" (1990: 145).

Opportunity and capacity can help to make teacher learning a natural part of a school's life. Rosabeth Moss Kanter (1977) has pointed out that using direct supervision and promulgating policies that standardize work processes or standardize outcomes do not so much control what people do as they control *what people cannot do*. That is a pretty scary proposition. It is one thing, for example, for a teacher to decide to use mimeographed worksheets when they are not appropriate in your grandchild's classroom and another thing when teachers are not able to give your grandchild the attention she or he may need because of excessively prescriptive testing, curriculum, and scheduling requirements. These and other "control over events" practices restrict the range of options available to teachers, heads, and even students. *Fewer options increase the likelihood that schools will not be able to respond satisfactorily to either the intellectual challenges and academic demands they face or the unique needs that students and parents face.* Both school and community, both teachers and students, both heads and policy makers lose as a result. Though it may be popular to mandate and prescribe, the reality is that the wholesale limiting of options for teachers, heads, and parents at the local school site is just bad educational policy.

As a result of her research, Kanter found that opportunity and capacity were essential for effective performance in complex work. In schools, opportunity refers to the perception that teachers and heads have for increasing knowledge, skills, and rewards. Do they have the opportunity to learn, to figure out ways in which challenging standards might be met, to respond to the needs of the children that they are responsible for? Do they have the opportunity to respond to increases in responsibility and increases in the challenges that they face? Capacity refers to the ability to get things done, to gather the resources that one needs in order to get things done, and to interact with others who can help get things done. Kanter warns that when opportunity and capacity are diminished, interest and excitement in one's work decrease.

Relying on Kanter's framework, Milbrey McLaughlin and Sylvia Mei-Ling Yee (1988) found that enhanced levels of opportunity and capacity resulted in teachers experiencing greater stimulation at work and higher levels of work motivation. They found, also, that a teacher's effectiveness was directly related to the opportunities that teacher had to develop basic competence, to experience challenge in teaching, to receive feedback about their importance, to get support for trying new things, and to get support for their own growth. Kanter and McLaughlin and Mei-Ling Yee suggest that there is much that leaders can do to directly improve opportunities for learning. But as mutual adjustment becomes even more important in schools and as the learning curves that will be needed become more steep, leaders will have to focus less and less on providing direct leadership and more and more on building substitutes for leadership into the very structure and culture of schooling itself.

Direct leadership is what leaders do when they work directly to enhance teacher learning. Substitutes for leadership are the structures, pathways, and norms leaders build that allow, encourage, and enhance teacher learning. Taking substitutes for leadership seriously means worrying just a little bit less about developing the intelligence of individual teachers and a little bit more about cultivating organizational intelligence.

The development of organizational intelligence

Think of it this way. If we can figure out how to make schools smarter as organizations, then it may be easier for people to learn and keep learning in the face of new knowledge and skill requirements. Smarter schools are more intelligent in an organizational sense. Gerald Skibbins

(1974) thinks of organizational intelligence as the sum of an organization's ability to perceive, to process information, to reason, to be imaginative, and to be motivated. The five are indicators of organizational intelligence. Some schools, for example, are more perceptive than others. In these schools the total amount of *perception* stored in the minds and hearts of heads, teachers, and others is greater. Some schools have figured out

"Smarter schools are more intelligent in an organizational sense."

how to increase their organizational *memory* as well. In these schools more people seem to know what is going on. More people have access to the information they need to be successful. More people are aware of their school's history and traditions. More people know about and have learned from previous mistakes than is the case in other schools. Some schools are able to *reason* better than others, show more *imagination*, and harness more *motivational energy* than others.

Schools that are perceptive are networked both internally and externally to sources of information that make them more aware of what they know, what the possibilities are, and what courses of action to take. They know where to find support, where the lines are that cannot be crossed, and where the degrees of freedom are greatest. Schools that have enhanced memory have developed data banks and have provided ways to make this information available to those who need it. Schools that have enhanced reason use data to help them understand better their circumstances and to make better decisions. This data is both hard and soft. Test scores, for example, are important and so are values and purposes, perceptions and beliefs. Schools that are imaginative have figured out ways to build into their structure and culture a considerable amount of freedom and flexibility. Schools with enhanced motivation are known as quality places to work and have committed teachers who want to be there.

The five indicators of organizational intelligence (perception, memory, reason, imagination, and motivation) correspond pretty well to the indicators that are considered in assessing individual intelligence. As the indicators strengthen, a school is able to increase its organizational intelligence. As the indicators weaken, that school's organizational intelligence decreases. When heads are able to enhance these indicators, they are providing substitutes for leadership in the sense that the indicators allow people in the school to behave more intelligently than would otherwise be the case. The more intelligently they behave, the less direct leadership they need from heads.

The question, of course, is how to enhance these indicators of intelligence in an organizational way. And the answer, according to Skibbins, is by manipulating certain organizational variables that affect the capacity of people to learn. Skibbins believes that there are a number of organizational variables that leaders can emphasize or de-emphasize and, depending upon how they are manipulated, the various indicators of organizational intelligence will be either enhanced or diminished. How one practices supervision, envisions decision-making, distributes authority, involves people, or communicates, for example, influences the extent to which the school and its people perceive, have a sense of memory, reason, are imaginative, and are motivated. These dimensions are shown in Table 6.1 and discussed below:

Span of control, the first organizational variable Skibbins discusses, is managerial jargon for the number of individuals who should "report" to each leader. The greater the number, the less likely that leaders will be directive and restrictive, thus allowing others to be more engaged in a wider range of the school's life. This engagement gives both leaders and others a wide-angle view of what is going on that increases perception. A wide span of control also enlarges everyone's scope of concern and involves them in a larger body of information about the school that increases memory across the board.

Leadership density, the second organizational variable, refers to the extent leadership responsibilities and practices are located deep among the faculty. The more people that are involved in leadership roles and responsibilities, the more dense is leadership in the schools. High leadership density increases the number of people who are engaged in the work of others, the number of people who are responsible for and engaged in the work of others, and thereby augments perception. High leadership density increases the number of people who are trusted with information and thereby enlarges memory. High leadership density increases the number of people concerned with decision-making and this augments reason. High leadership density increases the number of people who are exposed to new ideas and thus are more likely to generate even more new ideas, thereby enlarging imagination. And, finally,

Table 6.1 Making schools smarter by increasing organizational intelligence

| Indicators of intelligence | Organizational variables | | | |
	Span of control	Leadership density[a]	Time span for reaching goals and meeting deadlines	Degree of centralization in decision-making
Organizational perception	A large span of control enlarges a leader's breadth of view and thereby increases his or her perception.	Widely dispersed leadership increases the number of people responsible for school results and thereby augments perception.		Decentralized decision-making causes people throughout the organization to involve themselves in decision problems and thereby encourages perception.
Organizational memory	A wide span of control enlarges a leader's scope of concern and thereby involves the leader in a larger body of data and increases his or her memory.	Widely dispersed leadership increases the number of people entrusted with broad data and thereby enlarges memory.		Decentralized decision-making forces people throughout the organization to store data for future decision problems and thereby enlarges memory.
Organizational reason		Widely dispersed leadership increases the number of people concerned with decision-making and thereby augments reason.		Decentralized decision-making brings more minds into decision-making processes and thereby augments reasoning capacity in the organization.
Organizational imagination		Widely dispersed leadership increases the number of people employed to generate new ideas and thereby enlarges imagination.	A long time span allows employees to ponder problems and purposes at length, which permits imaginative ideas to arise in the mind.	Decentralized decision-making causes more minds to be engaged in problem solving and thereby increases the use of imagination.
Organizational motivation		Widely dispersed leadership increases the number of people with a career interest in the organization and thereby augments motivation.	A long time span enables the employee to accomplish major tasks of great importance and thereby furthers motivation.	Decentralized decision-making accords greater responsibilities for important work to more people and thereby increases motivation.

Source: This table, slightly adapted to fit the context of schools, appears by permission granted from Gerald J. Skibbins, P.O. Box 28, Sea Ranch, CA 95497, USA. It was originally published as Table A-1 "Artificial Intelligence and Organizational Variables" in Skibbins' book *Organizational Evolution: A Program for Managing Radical Change*, New York: AMACOM, 1974: 248–9.
Note: [a] *Leadership density* is substituted for *Ratio of Administrative to Productive Personnel* in the original.

Table 6.1 (cont.)

Organizational variables

Indicators of intelligence	Proportion of persons in one unit (department, grade level, team or school) having opportunity to interact with persons in other units	Quantity of formal rules	Specificity of goals, standards, and outcomes	Emphasizes values over direction[b]	Knowledge-based authority (vs. position based)
Organizational perception	A high proportion enlarges the exposure of people to activities throughout the organization and thereby increases perception.	A small quantity of rules makes people receptive to innovative ideas and thereby encourages perception.	A low specificity of goals, standards, and outcomes causes people to relate to overall aims of the organization and thereby promotes a greater breadth of perception among people.	An emphasis on values over directions leaves more people with the responsibility of managing their own activities and thereby encourages greater perception.	A high knowledge orientation places a premium on awareness among people and thereby promotes perception in the organization.
Organizational memory		A small quantity of rules broadens the scope of potentially relevant data and thereby enlarges the memory in the organization	A low specificity of goals, standards, and outcomes widens the base of data relevant to individuals and thereby increases memory.		A high knowledge orientation forces people to amass data in order to advance and thereby enlarges memory.
Organizational reason	A high proportion encourages the pooling of minds in response to problems to be solved and thereby augments reason.	A small quantity of rules exposes more procedures and practices to critical evaluation and thereby increases reason.	A low specificity of goals, standards, and outcomes causes people to concentrate their thoughts on the ultimate objectives of the organization and thereby augments effective reason.	An emphasis on values over directions leaves more people with problem-solving responsibilities of their own and thereby enlarges the exercise of reason.	A high knowledge orientation furthers logical thought activity among people in their effort to expand their knowledge and thereby increases reason.

Organizational imagination	A high proportion tends to draw many minds into problem-solving processes and thereby enlarges the exercise of imagination.	A small quantity of rules frees the minds of people for creative thinking and thereby encourages imagination.		An emphasis on values over directions allows greater freedom of action among people and thereby encourages the use of imagination.	A high knowledge orientation encourages growth in the data base as a stimulant to new ideas and thereby promotes imagination.
Organizational motivation	A high proportion makes people aware of their own places in the overall functions of the organization and thereby increases motivation.	A small quantity of rules permits people to exercise individual preferences and thereby increases motivation.	A low specificity of goals, standards, and outcomes involves people in the ultimate, major aims of the organization and thereby encourages higher identification and motivation.	An emphasis on values over directions promotes participatory management in the organization and thereby increases motivation.	

ᵇ *Emphasizes Values Over Directions* is substituted for *Advisory Content of Communications (vs. Orders)* in the original.

high leadership density increases the number of people who have an important stake in the school and its success, which augments motivation.

The third organizational variable is *time span* for reaching goals and determining success. When the time span is longer, people are able to ponder problems and reflect more on what is going on in the school and are able to accomplish things that are more important than would otherwise have been the case, enhancing both imagination and motivation. When the time span is too short, schools are encouraged to behave like corporations who are often forced to do almost anything to "get the next quarter's numbers up." Sometimes what they are forced to do in the short term jeopardizes their long-term capacity and profitability.

The fourth organizational variable, the degree of *centralization in decision-making*, impacts each of the indicators of organizational intelligence in important ways. Decentralization involves more people, gets more people into the information flow of the school thus increasing perception, brings more people together to ponder decisions thus increasing memory, causes more minds to be involved in problem solving thus increasing reason and imagination, and encourages more people to accept responsibility for what is going on thus enhancing motivation.

The fifth organizational variable is the *amount of interaction* that occurs across departments, teams, grade levels, and even schools. As interaction increases more people are involved more widely in what is going on in the school, ponder together problems to be solved, draw on the resources of each other to solve these problems, and build a higher sense of ownership in what is going on in the school. These, in turn, increase each of the five indicators of organizational intelligence.

The sixth organizational variable is *emphasis on formal rules*. How rules are understood and used by a school's leadership (or how rules are mandates from external sources) also influences the school's capacity to perceive, to develop its memory, to reason, to be imaginative, and to be motivated. Fewer rules increase the likelihood that people will be more receptive to ideas, broaden the extent to which people can be involved in contributing relevant data, expose rules to more critical evaluation, allow for more critical thinking, encourage imagination, and permit wider discretion.

Similar effects are sketched out for such organizational characteristics as *specificity of goals, standards, and outcomes*, the extent to which *values* are emphasized over directions, and the extent to which *knowledge-based authority* is used over position-based authority. With respect to goals, standards, and outcomes, less specificity, Skibbins maintains, helps increase organizational perception, memory, reason, and motivation thus enhancing organizational intelligence. Emphasizing values over directions and relying on knowledge-based authority are also broad contributors to organizational intelligence.

Some principles for organizing

Skibbins' conception of organizational intelligence may be more metaphorical than real. Nonetheless the idea is sufficiently powerful to be worth further consideration. Arguing that when organizations are structured in ways that enhance their "smartness" human intelligence increases just makes too much sense. Further, these ideas about substitutes for leadership and organizational intelligence may be directly transferable to the classroom. Are there classroom organizational features that enhance student perception, memory, reason, imagination, and motivation? I think so. With this thought in mind, here are some basic principles for organizing, whether we are talking about classrooms or schools (Sergiovanni 1995):

1   The principle of *cooperation* – When teachers cooperate with each other by working together, trying out ideas together, examining student work together, and helping each other, teaching and learning are enhanced. Further, cooperation helps overcome the effects of isolation that too often characterize teaching. In successful schools organizational structures enhance cooperation among teachers. Successful classrooms enhance cooperation among students.

2   The principle of *empowerment* – When teachers experience empowerment, this contributes to ownership, increased commitment, and motivation to work. When teachers feel like pawns rather than originators of their own behavior, they are likely to respond with reduced commitment, mechanical behavior, indifference, and even dissatisfaction and alienation. In successful schools organizational structures enhance empowerment among teachers. Similarly,

organizational structures in classrooms enhance empowerment among students.

3   The principle of *responsibility* – Most teachers want more responsibility. Responsibility enhances the importance and significance of their work and provides a tangible basis for recognizing their success. In successful schools organizational structures encourage teacher responsibility. Similarly, in successful classrooms organizational structures encourage student responsibility. Both forms of responsibility are keys to helping the school become a self-managing system.

4   The principle of *accountability* – Accountability is related to empowerment and responsibility. It is not likely that one is empowered or has real responsibility unless one is also accountable. Accountability provides a healthy measure of excitement, challenge, and importance that raises the stakes just enough so that achievement means something. In successful schools organizational structures allow teachers to be accountable for their decisions and achievements. Similarly, in successful classrooms there are organizational structures in place that encourage students to be accountable. When combined with empowerment, accountability helps the school become a community of responsibility (a theme discussed in Chapter 4).

5   The principle of *meaningfulness* – When teachers find their practice to be meaningful, teaching not only takes on special significance, but also provides teachers with feelings of intrinsic satisfaction. In successful schools organizational structures provide for meaningful work. Similarly, in successful classrooms organizational structures provide for students to experience meaningful work.

6   The principle of *ability–authority* – Thirty-five years ago the noted organizational theorist Victor Thompson (1961) stated that the major problem facing modern organizations is the growing gap which exists between those who have authority to act but not the necessary ability, and those who have ability to act but not the necessary authority. With today's knowledge explosion and increased specialization, what was once a gap seems more like a chasm. This ability–authority principle seeks to place those who have the ability to act in the forefront of decision-making. In successful schools organizational structures promote authority based on ability. In

schools where it is necessary for authority to be formally linked to one's position in the organizational hierarchy, day-by-day practice is characterized by formal and informal delegation of this authority to those with ability. Similarly, students often know more about certain topics than do adults (computers and dinosaurs, for example). This "ability–authority" gap needs to be breached by sharing authority with students.

As these organizational principles become common place in schools, they increase the capacity of everyone to respond more effectively to their problems. As a result, heads are able to lead more effectively, teaching is enhanced, and learning for both adults and students increases.

Going deeper

Throughout much of this chapter the emphasis has been on linking leadership with learning as a response to the complex adaptive systems nature of schools. Learning earns the center-stage position because it is a powerful way for schools to adapt, to stay ahead, and to invent new solutions. At the heart of any successful change is a change in culture which makes new goals, new initiatives, and new ways of behaving part of a school's norm structure. Forgetting the importance of culture and the importance of creating new norms leads to changes that resemble the proverbial "rearranging the chairs on the deck of the *Titanic*." But organizational factors count too and in important ways. Though we have no inventory of scientific findings to present, it seems clear that we can be much more deliberate in organizing schools in ways that enhance teacher learning and the learning of other adults. Further, as teachers learn more and as schools get smarter, students learn more too. But we cannot end this story here. We are missing the most important part: what can be done to help classrooms become more effective learning communities for students – particularly students who are usually thought of as not likely to do well?

Organizing classrooms for learning

Lauren Resnick of the Institute for Learning at the University of Pittsburgh has some ideas that can help answer the above question. She believes that effort counts in helping students learn – that intelligence is not immutable. Her research reveals that students who are treated as if they are intelligent become intelligent. When taught demanding content and when expected to explain and find connections as well as to memorize, they learn more and they learn more quickly. Resnick and her colleagues (1998, 1999) at the Institute for Learning have identified a core set of principles that seems to contribute to this learning:

CORE PRINCIPLES

1   *Organize for effort* An effort-based school replaces the assumption that aptitude determines what and how much students learn with the assumption that sustained and directed effort can yield high achievement for all students. Everything is organized to evoke and support this effort.

2   *Clear expectations* If we expect all students to learn at high levels, then we need to define what we expect students to learn. These expectations need to be clear – to school professionals, to parents, to the community, and, above all, to students themselves.

3   *Recognition of accomplishment* Clear recognition of authentic accomplishment is a hallmark of an effort-based school. This recognition can take the form of celebrations of work that meets standards or intermediate expectations.

4   *Fair and credible evaluations* Long-term effort by students calls for assessment practices that students find fair. Most importantly, tests, exams, and classroom assessments must be aligned to the standards and the curriculum being studied. Fair assessment also means using tests and exams that are graded against absolute standards rather than on a curve so students can clearly see the results of their learning efforts.

5   *Academic rigor in a thinking curriculum* Thinking and problem solving will be the "new basics" of the twenty-first century. But the common idea that we can teach thinking without a solid foundation of knowledge must be abandoned. So must the idea that we can teach knowledge without engaging

---

students in thinking. Knowledge and thinking must be intimately joined.

6 *Accountability talk* Talking with others about ideas and work is fundamental to learning. But not all talk sustains learning or creates intelligence. For classroom talk to promote learning, it must have certain characteristics that make it *accountable*. Accountability talk seriously responds to and further develops what others in the group have said. It puts forth and demands knowledge that is accurate and relevant to the issues under discussion.

7 *Socializing intelligence* Intelligent habits of mind are learned through the daily expectations placed on the learner. By calling on students to use the skills of intelligent thinking and accountability talk, and by holding them responsible for doing so, educators can teach intelligence.

8 *Learning as apprenticeship* For many centuries, most people learned by working alongside an expert who modeled skilled practice and guided novices as they created authentic products or performances. This kind of apprenticeship learning allowed learners to acquire the complex interdisciplinary knowledge, practical abilities, and appropriate forms of social behavior that went with high levels of skilled performance . . . Much of the power of apprenticeship learning can be brought into schooling through appropriate use of extended projects and presentations, and by organizing learning environments so that complex thinking and production are modeled and analyzed.

(excerpted from Resnick 1999: 40)

The challenge of leadership

As part of a study of perceptions of good leadership by Danish, English, and Scottish teachers, John MacBeath and his colleagues Leif Moos, Pat Mahony, and Jenny Reeves (1998) have identified five "definitions" of school leadership:

1 Leadership means having a clear personal vision of what you want to achieve.

2   Good leaders are in the thick of things, working alongside their col-
    leagues.
3   Leadership means respecting teachers' autonomy, protecting them
    from extraneous demands.
4   Good leaders look ahead, anticipate change and prepare people for
    it so that it doesn't surprise or disempower them.
5   Good leaders are pragmatic. They are able to grasp the realities of
    the political and economic context and they are able to negotiate
    and compromise.

(Moos, Mahony, and Reeves in MacBeath 1998: 63)

The researchers found that English teachers listed the first definition of
a strong leader with a personal vision as their top choice, even though
one in four teachers rated this definition as the worst. Danish teachers
were inclined to favor the fourth definition – a forward-looking leader
who would empower teachers to prepare for the future. Scottish teachers preferred definitions 2 and 1. Within every group, however, each of
the definitions was preferred by some of the teachers suggesting that
leadership, broadly conceived, is about many things. Though given different weights, the qualities of leadership suggested by the five
definitions find their way into the practice of most heads.

   In a related study Christopher Day and his colleagues identify a sixth
definition as follows:

6   Good leaders are informed by, and communicate, clear sets of per-
    sonal and educational values which represent their moral purposes
    for the school.

(Day *et al.* 2000: 165)

The heads in this study were able to create a fabric of reciprocal relationships and mutual support that tied everyone together in a sensible
pattern of action on behalf of their schools. The heads cultivated professional dialogue among teachers and placed a high premium upon
their own professional development as part of a broad and deep commitment to learning for everyone. They developed professional and
intellectual capital by helping their schools become inquiring communities committed to rigorous and authentic learning. They practiced
what Day and his colleagues call "post-tranformational leadership" – a

values-led leadership based on firm convictions, personal integrity, and commitment to action. These European findings have a ring of familiarity when one examines the leadership scene in Canada, the USA, Singapore, Australia, and other developed countries. In the researchers' words:

> The heads in this study were effective because they held and communicated clear vision and values. They empowered staff by developing a climate of collaboration, by applying high standards to themselves and others and monitoring these, by seeking the support of various influential groups within the school community, by keeping 'ahead of the game' through ensuring that they had a national strategic view of forthcoming changes, and by managing their own personal and professional selves. They managed tensions between dependency and autonomy, between caution and courage, between maintenance and development . . . their focus was always upon the betterment of the young people and staff who worked in their schools. They remained also, often against all the odds, enthusiastic and committed to learning. Their strength was demonstrated in their hopefulness at all times . . .
>
> (ibid.: 177–8)

These researchers are on to something important. Granted, leadership is hard to pin down. It takes many forms. The same leadership behaviors have different meanings in different contexts. Idealism is important. A pragmatic bent oriented to action makes this idealism real. The art of leadership is found in the steady balance that leaders bring to their practice. It all works because of deeply held convictions and commitment to action. In short, effective leaders base their practice on ideas and have the grit to act on these ideas.

Perhaps top on any list of leadership virtues is humility. It is dangerous for leaders to think of themselves as providers of solutions that save the day. In reality heads and teachers are faced with many problems but few solutions. Under these circumstances leadership is a quest, a search for some light, a struggle to keep moving in a direction that makes sense for children, their parents, and their community. Leadership is not a given, is not an answer, is not a fixed destination. The more schools resemble complex adaptive systems, the more likely that successful leadership will depend on the leader's ability to ask for and receive the help of everyone involved in the school. Tom Morris raises the humility question by noting that leaders are little more than "dust and ashes." Thus they must ask themselves:

> What can I alone accomplish?. . . If I can open myself to what is out there in the world beyond the boundaries of my own small self, if I can lower myself into a state of humble openness to receive what others have to offer, then they are more likely to pour themselves out *into me* and help me accomplish the most difficult and the most worthy of tasks.
>
> (1997: 215)

If we heed his advice, then we will have discovered the secret of leadership.

QUESTIONS FOR FURTHER EXPLORATION

1   "External reviews should be granted in the school's promises
    and school improvements plans."
    How adequate a model is this for the role of external
    inspection?

2   "One way to engender trust is through public disclosure."
    How valid a statement is this in your experience? What
    assumptions underpin it?

3   What is meant in practice by probabilities rather than events?
    How can this provide a basis for development, or improve-
    ment, planning?

4   Consider the five definitions of leadership below. Mark with
    a tick the definition closest to your own preferred definition.
    Mark with a cross the one furthest away.

	1 The headteacher should have a clear view of what makes it a good school and be able to inspire people to make it happen.	
	2 A good headteacher leads by example. He/she should work in the classroom alongside the teachers and encourage them to take responsibility for improving things.	
	3 Good schools let teachers get on with the job and protect them from too many outside pressures.	
	4 A good headteacher should know what is going on and be able to look ahead and make sure staff are ready for what is coming so that they are able to deal with change confidently and in a planned way.	
	5 Good leaders are pragmatic. They are able to grasp the realities of the political and economic context. They know how to negotiate and when to compromise and how to get the best out of the system for the benefit of their own school.	

7 Leadership in the real world

A postscript by Richard Middleton

Americans have long espoused education as fundamental to the perpetuation of a democratic society and a vibrant economy. Our schools have been "instruments of the people, chartered to do the important work of our country . . . [and] as much a foundation for American democracy as the Constitution and the Bill of Rights" (Mathews 1996: 11). Yet while Americans believe that education is essential to the betterment of this society, great differences of opinion still exist about what constitutes an excellent education.

We continually debate issues that range from financial equity to social policy, from local and state standards to national testing, and from education as public obligation to education as private enterprise. This lack of agreement has created an unfocused vision about the purpose and future of education in this country. Glickman noted, "unfortunately, part of the reason why schools are such easy targets for criticism is that their goals are so diffuse and fragmented" (1993: 7).

As a consequence, public education's diverse stakeholders have often promoted differing and conflicting solutions which many times are embedded in political agendas rather than in student success. The result has been swings in law and policy at the local, state, and national level as lawmakers rush to enact their education "solutions du jour" for quality schools. In the past, this menu approach to schooling has included such issues as class size, phonics, traditional math, school uniforms, and zero tolerance, each of which has value, but enacted in isolation precludes truly systemic reform. At times, it seems that Americans truly believe their governments are able to enact laws and policies that will ensure every schoolchild is strong, beautiful, and as in Garrison Keillor's

Lake Wobegon, "above average." Educators are simply left to cope with the results.

As educators we now find ourselves in a time where educational progress is increasingly measured in terms of test results based on highly regulated standards of curriculum. Much of the current education debate focuses on the validity of these high stakes accountability systems. A cursory review of the education literature provides opinions from experts with competing points of view who are advocates for the extremes of the present debate. Some articles strongly assert the need for rigorous accountability systems with the intent of punishing low-performing school systems, while others argue to abandon high stakes testing in favor of more creative portfolio exhibits. Debates such as these become divisive for a community, and ultimately are of limited assistance to educators.

As a practicing superintendent, what I crave most for school leaders is discussion at the center of important issues. For example, rather than advocating or berating high stakes testing, leaders must focus on the primary mission of improving education for all students. For educators in the field, the real issue is not whether to test young people, but how to best use the test results to improve instruction. While test scores should never be the method by which our society totally defines the social and intellectual worth of an individual, a school, or a community, it must be acknowledged that test taking is a necessary, lifelong skill. Today's students will face tests many times in the years after graduation, as examinations are required in all areas of life including applications for a driver's license, entrance to graduate school, or a career promotion.

What must not be overlooked is that the national standards movement is actually changing the focus of education reform. It is now possible to measure the equity of schools by increases in the levels of student achievement instead of indicators such as simple comparisons of spending per student or ratios of counselors to students (Odden and Picus 2000). As we set our expectations higher for all students, policy makers must determine the most efficient and effective methods of *successfully* addressing the diverse needs of students. We must now concern ourselves with engaging groups of students with ever widening differences and demonstrating that all can achieve higher levels of learning. Linda Darling-Hammond (1997) argues that learning to high standards is the right of all children, and the future of public schools depends on this success. As has been demonstrated before, parents and other tax-payers will not oblige schools strapped for money without credible evidences of student growth in achievement.

Educators must become more sophisticated in their ability to develop capacity for teaching and leading in our schools, and we must be equipped for change. The reality is that schools are not constants; they are inhabited by heads, teachers, and children who occupy the building for only a brief period of time. To be effective today, school leaders cannot depend solely on leadership by command and control and the strength of their personality. Command and control leadership requires that teachers only focus for brief periods, and it is ultimately draining to a school community. When the leader leaves, the school's energy and spirit quickly dissipate. By contrast, effective school leadership is, as Sergiovanni writes, "primarily an act of trust" (1992: 139), and not so much a matter of problem solving as it is sustaining a climate of learning and a culture of opportunity for students and teachers. School heads are charged to create a community of moral purpose with the capacity to reinvent itself to meet challenges.

In their research on visionary, enduring companies, Collins and Porras found that for these organizations, "the only truly reliable source of stability [was] a strong inner core and the willingness to change and adapt everything except that core" (1994: xx). As schools are charged with caring for children, they may be considered moral institutions. School leaders must direct efforts toward the core purpose of increasing the ability of all children and preparing students for the future.

It must also be noted that professionals working alone cannot possibly design programs and systems that can cope with such complexity. Shulman states that there is a "distinctive wisdom about teaching among practicing teachers," (1997: 91) but that this wisdom is often isolated and unvoiced. He asserts that when teachers work in lonely circumstances, it makes it difficult for them to articulate what they know and share what they have learned with peers. The role of the head, then, is to create a school culture of reflective practice in which understandings achieved during the course of practice are nurtured and not forgotten. As a superintendent, I applaud heads who have the skill to build the capacity of teachers to work together to absorb changes in mandates and convert these to creative teaching experiences for children that improve student success and achievement.

It has long been my experience that the most successful schools are those in which teachers feel a sense of ownership and responsibility. Heads who are able to develop small teams of teachers who share a common group of students and common goals are highly effective. Whether it is grouping elementary students into families of learners, teaming at the middle school level, or designing magnet school programs at the high school level, the common element for success is a caring, focused group of teachers and students who trust one another and work together as a community with a common purpose.

> Community encompasses the relationships that occur day-to-day. It involves teachers, students, families, neighborhoods and beyond. It is built around shared experiences involving common struggles, successes, and failures, [and] is sustained by structures that promote dialogue about students, learning, teaching, curriculum, expectations, and results.
>
> (Lieberman and Miller 1999: 10)

For the last several years, educators in Texas have begun their school year in an environment of ever-increasing standards of accountability. Schools and school districts are ranked by test scores and dropout rates analyzed by four student subgroups, Anglo, Hispanic, African American, Economically Disadvantaged. The goal of this system is to ensure that educators have the same expectations for all students. All of these elements create a complex matrix that classifies schools and school districts under four categories based on annual test and dropout results.

The goal of the Texas system is laudable in that it sets higher standards for all children, but such a ranking system has the potential to create anomalies and categorize a total school as low performing based on the thinnest margins of dropout rate or test scores by one subpopulation group of students. A system with such complexity and demands calls for leaders with the skill to build leadership capacity within the school by encouraging teacher interdependence and maximizing opportunities for teacher learning. In a study of schools in south Texas, Thomas (1999) found that the head's leadership was essential in providing the impetus and the organizational structure that resulted in the transformation of the school staff into a professional learning community.

The role of leadership is to maintain the school community's energy and nurture the core purpose of increasing the ability of all children and preparing students for the future. It is with that role in mind that I offer the following eight principles for leadership, borrowed heavily from a variety of experiences in both the education and business worlds. Leaders must remember that their words and stance on issues impact others in both large and small ways. These principles are meant to be a practical guide to developing leaders who are able to create school communities that thrive in complex times of change.

Leadership for excellence

1 Focus on instructional excellence

Schools are moral institutions, and school leaders have a moral obligation to see that children are well served, and that teachers are supported in their efforts in behalf of children. A head's first role is to engage teachers in determining and articulating a vision of excellence for all students. The head's charge is to align the school's resources with the instructional priorities. Communication in the school should include conversation about school issues and the needs of children with meetings to analyze data and plan lessons. The head's challenge is to provide focus for the curriculum and structure opportunities and time for teachers to: (1) plan their lessons; (2) measure what students learn; (3) scrutinize the results in order to evaluate instructional efforts; and (4) develop appropriate improvement initiatives.

2 Value connections

When teachers and heads consider themselves to be a community, they engage in dialogue and discussion about teaching and learning. While colleagueship and collaboration will not solve every school problem, collective conversation about how teachers teach and how students learn is a critical component of school improvement. As a superintendent, my goal is to develop heads with the expertise and capacity to encourage teachers to work together to acquire the knowledge, strategies, and techniques necessary to propel the school to high performing status.

Schools at risk weaken an entire district. It is incumbent on a district's central office staff to support the work of the head and teachers by providing the expertise, guidance, and strategies required for the school to attain its goals for student achievement. With a purposeful central office staff, it is possible to make a significant contribution toward the effectiveness of a school staff.

3 Understand the ground

To understand the ground means for a leader to develop awareness of what is going on both inside and outside the school's community. Heads should have good data about the working relationships of teachers and other staff members. Time must be preserved for celebrating successes and for identifying and working through organizational issues. Time well spent in this area will develop trust and provide the school staff with encouragement and support through the more difficult days.

Superintendents and heads must also spend time with publics outside the school. Leaders must understand how others view the school and district in the larger context of the community of the city and state. The more educators learn the merits of others' viewpoints, the more opportunities will arise to involve schools in solving large community issues. Educators must always remember that schools do not survive and thrive in isolation. Public school leaders are public servants, and depend on tax revenues to exist. Our challenge is to keep our communities involved and supportive of the mission of public schools.

4 Envelop a problem

Leaders must internalize the "map" or vision for the school community, and are charged with anticipating upcoming problems, interruptions, and changes to the school's instructional program.

As school staff members develop one-, five-, and ten-year plans to meet student needs, heads must take care to understand current issues and their constraints, and not to discount any potential challenges to established strategies for success. During my career, I have found that instructional and interpersonal problems are seldom solved with a single solution or "silver bullet." To ensure curricular continuity and community success, leaders must envelop problematic issues by considering them from every angle and addressing them at multiple levels in a myriad of ways.

5 Be resilient

Every successful organization has a person or persons who re-energizes those around them with their enthusiasm for the mission before them. These individuals are the "flag bearers" that provide a rallying point for the group when times are confusing or difficult. Leaders in schools must have the passion necessary to always be reliable for others and tirelessly persistent to the goal. These leaders must also have the maturity and wisdom to cultivate as many "flag bearers" as possible.

6 Encourage leadership

A vital role for leaders is to mentor peers as potential leaders. By sharing with each other, leaders develop support groups and "think tanks" to explore new ideas. These conversations and relationships provide a method for leaders to overcome the loneliness and isolation leaders may experience during difficult times.

A successful school system has a formalized procedure for identifying and nurturing future leaders. A school district would greatly benefit from an aggressive recruitment and preparation of individuals each year who would be able to assume leadership positions as they became available. Such a training system would provide continuity of leaders who understand the organization and share its goals.

7 Enjoy the challenge

Sergiovanni has argued that educating youth today is a complex endeavor that defies singular or even long-lasting solutions. After ten years as a superintendent, I truly appreciate how profound his observation is. However, rather than frustrating I find this challenge both enjoyable and energizing. Understanding and liking the ramifications of one's occupation are essential to being successful. Many times the rewards of service are long term and rather evasive, but no one can discount the importance of such efforts. To be an effective school leader, one must truly have a passion for helping people learn and must be convinced that teaching can make a very real difference to all groups of students.

8 Continue to learn

This principle for leadership must seem to be the most obvious. However, continuing to learn means more than seeking new degrees or certifications for job advancement or staff development. It means that leaders must strive to be model learners. We must continue to read, and engage in discussions about all matter of subjects as well as the most recent theories of learning. As leaders we must question our current practices and be willing to research new findings about our profession. We must never feel that we have learned enough or have "progressed" beyond the point of being a learner. Learning is truly a lifelong experience, and cannot be thought of as simply a destination.

Leaders and leadership make the difference in establishing and maintaining successful schools. As Gardner wrote, "the light we sought is shining still . . . the great ideas still beckon – freedom, equality, justice, the release of human possibilities" (1990: xi). We must embrace the complexity of the education world today, and not become disheartened by change. Our focus and goal must remain for children to become empowered for success in the future because of the challenging education their schools made available for them.

Notes

1 The real context for leadership

1 This discussion follows closely T.J. Sergiovanni "Value-Driven Schools: The Amoeba Theory," in Harry Walberg and John Lane (eds) (1989) *Organizing for Learning: Toward the 21st Century*, Reston, VA: National Association of Secondary School Principals. ©T.J. Sergiovanni (1988).

2 Leading with ideas

1 This discussion of theories closely follows T.J. Sergiovanni (1994) "The Roots of School Leadership," *Principal*, 74, 2: 7–9.

3 New leadership, roles, and competencies

1 This discussion of leadership and change is drawn from T.J. Sergiovanni (2000) "Changing Change: Toward a Design Science and Art," *Journal of Educational Change*, 1, 1: 57–75. ©T.J. Sergiovanni (1999).

4 Leading communities of responsibility

1 Academic press, a term commonly used in school effectiveness research, refers to the extent a school emphasizes academic achievement. Sebring and Bryk (1996) point out that schools with high levels of academic press expect students to work on intellectually challenging tasks, come to school prepared to learn, and complete all assignments.

5 School character, school effectiveness, and layered standards

1 State refers to states in the USA and other countries, provinces and similar jurisdictions, and federal governments.
2 This discussion of standards draws on Chapters 5 and 6 "Layered Standards and Shared Accountability" and "Whole Child, Whole School,

Holistic Assessment" in T.J. Sergiovanni (2000) *The Lifeworld of Leadership: Creating Culture, Community, and Personal Meaning in Our Schools*, San Francisco: Jossey-Bass; and T.J. Sergiovanni (2000) "Standards and the Lifeworld of Leadership," *The School Administrator*, Vol. 57, No. 8.

References

Ames, C. (1984) "Competitive, Cooperative and Individualistic Goal Structures: A Cognitive-Motivational Analysis," in R. Ames and C. Ames (eds) *Research on Motivation in Education*, (Volume 1), Orlando, FL: Academic Press, 177–207.

Ames, C. (1992) "Achievement Goals and the Classroom Motivational Climate," in D. H. Shunk and J. L. Meece (eds) *Student Perception in the Classroom*, Hillsdale, NJ: Erlbaum.

Ancess, J. (1996) *Outside/Inside, Inside/Outside: Developing and Implementing the School Quality Review*, New York: National Center for Restructuring Education, Schools and Teaching.

Aristotle (1962) *Nicomachean Ethics*, trans. M. Ostwald, Indianapolis: Bobbs-Merrill.

Banner, J. M., Jr. and Cannon, H. C. (1999) "A Student's Best Lesson: Learning is Not a Passive – or a One-Way – Enterprise," *Education Week*, 20 October, 60.

Barth, R. S. (1980) *Run School Run*, Cambridge, MA: Harvard University Press.

Barth, R. S. (1990) *Improving Schools From Within*, San Francisco: Jossey-Bass.

Barton, P. E. (1999) *Too Much Testing of the Wrong Kind; Too Little of the Right Kind in K-12 Education*, Policy Information Center Research Division, Princeton, NJ: Educational Testing Service.

Bennis, W. (1989) *Why Leaders Can't Lead: The Unconscious Conspiracy Continues*, San Francisco: Jossey-Bass.

Bennis, W. and Nanus, B. (1985) *Leaders: The Strategies for Taking Charge*, New York: Harper & Row.

Bryk, A. S. and Driscoll, M. E. (1988) *The School as Community: Theoretical Foundations, Contextual Influences and Consequences for Teachers and Students*, Madison, WI: National Center for Effective Secondary Schools.

Bryk, A. S., Sebring, P. B., Kerbow, D., Rollow, S. and Easton, J. Q. (1998) *Charting Chicago School Reform: Democratic Localism as a Lever for Change*, Boulder, CO: Westview Press.

Burns, J. M. (1978) *Leadership*, New York: Harper & Row.

Byrne, J. A. (1999) "The Global Corporation Becomes the Leaderless Corporation," *Business Week*, 30 August, 88–90.

Carey, G. W. and Frohnen, B. (eds) (1998) *Community and Tradition: Conservative Perspectives on the American Experience*, Lanham, MD: Rowman & Littlefield Publishers.

Clinchy, E. (1995) "Why are we Restructuring?" *New Schools, New Communities*, 11, 3: 7–12.

Cohen, M. D. and March, J. G. (1974) *Leadership and Ambiguity: The American College President*, New York: McGraw-Hill.

Cohen, M. D., March, J. G. and Olsen, J. P. (1972) "A Garbage Can Model of Organizational Choice," *Administrative Science Quarterly*, 17, 1: 1–25.

Coleman, J. S. (1988) "Social Capital in the Creation of Human Capital," *American Journal of Sociology*, 94, Supplement: S95–S120.

Coleman, J. S. (1990) *Foundations of Social Theory*, Cambridge, MA: Harvard University Press.

Collins, J. C. and Porras, J. I. (1994) *Built to Last: Successful Habits of Visionary Companies*, New York: Harper Business.

Cuban, L. (1998) "A Tale of Two Schools," *Education Week*, 28 January, 33.

Darling-Hammond, L. (1997) *The Right to Learn*, San Francisco: Jossey-Bass.

Day, C., Harris, A., Hadfield, M., Tolley, H., and Beresford, J. (2000) *Leading Schools in Times of Change*, Buckingham: Open University Press.

Durkheim, E. (1960) "Rousseau's Social Contract," in *Montesquieu and Rousseau: Forerunners of Sociology*, trans. R. Manheim, Ann Arbor: University of Michigan Press, 65–138.

Dwyer, D. (1989) "School Climate Starts at the Curb," *School Climate – The Principal Difference*, Monograph Series #1, The Connecticut Principals' Academy, Hartford, CT, 1–26.

Etzioni, A. (1989) "Humble Decision Making," *Harvard Business Review*, 67, 4: 122–6.

Etzioni, A. (1993) *The Spirit of Community: Rights, Responsibilities, and the Communitarian Agenda*, New York: Crown.

Etzioni, A. (ed.) (1995) *New Communitarian Thinking: Persons, Virtues, Institutions, and Communities*, Charlottesville: University Press of Virginia.

Etzioni, A. (1996/97) "The Community of Communities," *The Responsive Community*, 7, 1: 21–32.

Etzioni, A. (1999) *The Limits of Privacy*, New York: Basic Books.

Freedman, D. H. (1992) "Is Management Still a Science?" *Harvard Business Review*, 70, 6: 26–38.

Fullinwider, R. K. (1986) "Civic Education and Traditional Values," *Philosophy and Public Policy*, 6, 3.

Gardner, H. (1995) *Leading Minds: An Anatomy of Leadership*, New York: Basic Books.

Gardner, J. W. (1986a) *The Heart of the Matter: Leader-Constituent Interaction*, Leadership Papers 3, Washington, DC: INDEPENDENT SECTOR.

Gardner, J. W. (1986b) *Leadership and Power*, Leadership Papers 4, Washington, DC: INDEPENDENT SECTOR.

Gardner, J. W. (1990) *On Leadership*, New York: The Free Press.

Geertz, C. (1973) *The Interpretation of Cultures*, New York: Basic Books.

Glickman, C. D. (1993) *Renewing America's Schools: A Guide for School-based Action*, San Francisco: Jossey-Bass.

Greenfield, T. B. (1984) "Leaders and Schools: Willfulness and Nonnatural Order in Organizations," in T. J. Sergiovanni and J .E. Corbally (eds) *Leadership and Organizational Culture*, Urbana: University of Illinois Press, 142–69.

Habermas, J. (1987) *The Theory of Communicative Action, Vol. 2: Lifeworld and System: A Critique of Functionalist Reason*, trans. T. McCarthy, Boston, MA: Beacon Press.

Hackman, J. R. (1986) "The Psychology of Self-Management in Organizations," in M. S. Pallak and R. Perloff (eds) *Psychology and Work: Productivity, Change , and Employment*, Washington, DC: American Psychological Association, 89–125.

Hargreaves, A. and Fullan, M. (1998) "What's Worth Fighting For Out There? Guidelines for Principals," Toronto: Ontario Institute for Studies in Education at the University of Toronto.

Hayes, R. H. (1985) "Strategic Planning – Forward in Reverse?" *Harvard Business Review*, 63, 6: 111–19.

Heifetz, R. A. (1994) *Leadership Without Easy Answers*, Cambridge, MA: Harvard University Press.

Henderson, A. T. and Berla, N. (eds) (1994) *A New Generation of Evidence: The Family is Critical to Student Achievement*, Washington, DC: Center for Law and Education.

Hill, P. T. and Celio, M. B. (1998) *Fixing Urban Schools*, Washington, DC: Brookings Institution Press.

Hill, P. T., Foster, G. E. and Gendler, T. (1990) *High Schools with Character*, Santa Monica, CA: RAND Corporation.

Hoff, D. J. (1998) "At Long Last, California Board Adopts Standards for All Core Disciplines," *Education Week*, 21 October, 12.

Homans, G. C. (1950) *The Human Group*, New York: Harcourt Brace.

Interfaith Education Fund (1998) *Alliance Concept Paper*, The Foundation, Austin, Texas.

Kanter, R. M. (1977) *Men and Women of the Corporation*, New York: Basic Books.

Lambert, L. (1998) "How to Build Leadership Capacity," *Educational Leadership*, 55, 7: 17–19.

Lambert, L. and others (1995) *The Constructivist Leader*, New York: Teachers College Press.

Langer, S. K. (1957) *Philosophy in a New Key: A Study in the Symbolism of Reason, Rite, and Art*, Cambridge, MA: Harvard University Press.

Lieberman, A. and Miller, L. (1984) *Teachers, Their World, and Their Work*, Alexandria, VA: Association for Supervision and Curriculum Development.

Lieberman, A. and Miller, L. (1999) *Teachers – Transforming Their World and Their Work*, New York: Teachers College Press.

Lightfoot, S. L. (1983) *The Good High School: Portraits of Character and Culture*, New York: Basic Books.

Lipham, J. M. (1964) "Leadership and Administration," in D. E. Griffiths (ed.) *Behavioral Science and Educational Administration*, The Sixty-Third Yearbook of the National Society for the Study of Education, Part II, Chicago: The Society, 119–41.

McCall, M. W., Jr. and Lombardo, M. M. (1978) "Where Else Can We Go?" in McCall and Lombardo (eds) *Leadership: Where Else Can We Go?* Durham, NC: Duke University Press, 151–66.

McDonnell, L. M. and Elmore, R. F. (1987) "Getting the Job Done: Alternative Policy Instruments," *Educational Evaluation and Policy Analysis*, 9, 2: 133–52.

McLaughlin, M., Mei-Ling Yee, S. (1988) "School as a Place to Have a Career," in A. Lieberman (ed.) *Building a Professional Culture in Schools*, New York: Teachers College Press.

Maehr, M. L. and Midgley, C. (1996) *Transforming School Cultures*, Boulder, CO: Westview Press.

March, J. G. (1984) "How We Talk and How We Act: Administrative Theory and Administrative Life," in T. J. Sergiovanni and J. E. Corbally (eds) *Leadership and Organizational Culture*, Urbana: University of Illinois Press, 18–35.

Mathews, D. (1996) *Is There a Public for Public Schools?* Dayton, OH: Kettering Foundation Press.

Midgley, C. and Wood, S. (1993) "Beyond Site-Based Management: Empowering Teachers to Reform Schools," *Phi Delta Kappan*, 75, 3: 245–52.

Mintzberg, H. (1979) *The Structuring of Organizations*, Englewood Cliffs, NJ: Prentice-Hall.

Moos, L., Mahony, P. and Reeves, J. (1998) "What Teachers, Parents, Governors and Pupils Want from Their Heads," in J. MacBeath (ed.) *Effective School Leadership: Responding to Change*, London: Paul Chapman Publishing, 60–79.

Morris, T. (1997) *If Aristotle Ran General Motors*, New York: Henry Holt.

Morse, R. A. (1992) Research Review: "Honey Bees Have Solved the Problem of Finding and Exploiting the Best Food Source Available. Exciting News For Bee Keepers, Business Schools, and Psychologists," *Gleanings in Bee Culture*, January.

Newmann, F. M., Lopez, G., and Bryk, A. S. (1998) *The Quality of Intellectual Work in Chicago's Schools: A Baseline Report*, Chicago: Consortium on Chicago Schools

Research. Online. Available HTTP: http://www.consortium-chicago.org/html_web_store_3.0/html/intellect_desc.html (22 November 1999).

Newmann, F. M., Secada, W. G. and Wehlage, G. G. (1995) *A Guide to Authentic Instruction and Assessment: Vision, Standards and Scoring*, Madison: Wisconsin Center for Education Research.

Newmann, F. M. and Wehlage, G. G. (1995) *Successful School Restructuring*, Madison, WI: Center on Organization and Restructuring of Schools.

Nias, J., Southworth, G. and Yeomans, R. (1989) *Staff Relationships in the Primary School: A Study of Organizational Cultures*, London: Cassell.

Nothwehr, D. (1998) *Mutuality: A Formal Norm for Christian Social Ethics*, San Francisco: Catholic Scholars Press.

Odden, A. R. and Picus, L. O. (2000) *School Finance: A Policy Perspective*, Boston, MA: McGraw-Hill.

Olson, S. (1998) "Science Friction," *Education Week*, 30 September, 25–9.

Peters, T. J. and Waterman, R. H., Jr. (1982) *In Search of Excellence: Lessons from America's Best-Run Companies*, New York: Harper & Row.

Pondy, L.R. (1978) "Leadership is a Language Game," in M. W. McCall, Jr. and M. M. Lombardo (eds) *Leadership: Where Else Can We Go?* Durham, NC: Duke University Press, 87–101.

Putnam, R. D. (2000) *Bowling Alone: The Collapse and Revival of American Community*, New York: Simon & Schuster.

Quinn, J. B. (1981) "Formulating Strategy One Step at a Time," *Journal of Business Strategy*, 1, 3.

Resnick, L. B. (1999) "Making America Smarter: A Century's Assumptions About Innate Ability Give Way to a Belief in the Power of Effort," *Education Week*, 16 June, 38–40.

Resnick, L. B. and Hall, M. W. (1998) "Learning Organizations for Sustainable Education Reform," *Daedalus*, 127, 4: 89–118.

Roethlisberger, F. J. and Dickson, W. J. (1939) *Management and the Worker*, Cambridge, MA: Harvard University Press.

Rousseau, M. F. (1991) *Community: The Tie that Binds*, Lanham, MD: University Press of America.

Sa, Sophia (2000) "The More You Give Away," *The Panasonic Partnership Program*, a newsletter of the Panasonic Foundation, 1, 9: 1.

Sacks, J. (1997) "Rebuilding Civil Society: A Biblical Perspective," *Responsive Community*, 7, 1: 11–20.

Sandham, J. L. (2000) "Florida Cabinet Revises School Accountability System," *Education Week*, 12 January, 19.

Saphier J. and King, M. (1985) "Good Seeds Grow in Strong Cultures," *Educational Leadership*, 42, 6: 67–74.

Sarason, S. B. (1990) *The Predictable Failure of Educational Reform*, San Francisco: Jossey-Bass.

Schlosberg, J. (1993) "An Attraction to the 'Properly Complicated,'" *Rochester Review*, Fall Issue.

Schön, D. A. (1987) *Educating the Reflective Practitioner*, San Francisco: Jossey-Bass.

Sebring, P. B. and Bryk, A. S. (1996) "Student-Centered Learning Climate," in Sebring and others, *Charting Reform in Chicago: The Students Speak*, a report sponsored by the Consortium on Chicago School Research, Chicago, IL: University of Chicago.

Sergiovanni, T. J. (1984) "Leadership and Excellence in Schooling," *Educational Leadership*, 41, 5: 4–13.

Sergiovanni, T. J. (1987) "Will We Ever Have a TRUE Profession?" *Educational Leadership*, 44, 8: 44–9.

Sergiovanni, T. J. (1992) *Moral Leadership: Getting to the Heart of School Improvement*, San Francisco: Jossey-Bass.

Sergiovanni, T. J. (1994a) *Building Community in Schools*, San Francisco: Jossey-Bass.

Sergiovanni, T. J. (1994b) "The Roots of School Leadership," *Principal*, 74, 2: 6–9.

Sergiovanni, T. J. (1995) *The Principalship: A Reflective Practice Perspective*, 3rd edition, Boston, MA: Allyn and Bacon.

Sergiovanni, T. J. (1996) *Leadership for the Schoolhouse: How Is It Different? Why Is It Important?* San Francisco: Jossey-Bass.

Sergiovanni, T. J. (2000) *The Lifeworld of Leadership: Creating Culture, Community, and Personal Meaning in Our Schools*, San Francisco: Jossey-Bass.

Shouse, R. C. (1996) "Academic Press and a Sense of Community: Conflict, Congruence, and Implications for Student Achievement," *Social Psychology of Education*, 1: 47–68.

Shulman, L. S. (1989) "Teaching Alone, Learning Together: Needed Agendas for the New Reforms," in T. J. Sergiovanni and J. H. Moore (eds) *Schooling for Tomorrow: Directing Reforms to Issues that Count*, Boston, MA: Allyn and Bacon, 166–87.

Shulman, L. S. (1997) "Professional Development: Learning from Experience," in B. S. Kogan (ed.) *Common Schools, Uncommon Futures: A Working Consensus for School Renewal*, New York: Teachers College Press, 89–106.

Skibbins, G. (1974) *Organizational Evolution: A Program for Managing Radical Change*, New York: AMACOM.

Sowell, T. (1999) "Motive for Change can be Self-Serving," *San Antonio Express-News*, 22 June, 5B.

Starratt, R. J. (1973) "Contemporary Talk on Leadership: Too Many Kings in the Parade?" *Notre Dame Journal of Education*, 4, 1: 5–14.

Steinbeck, J. (1962) *The Log from the Sea of Cortez*, New York: Viking Press.

Sternberg, R. (1996) "What is Successful Intelligence?" *Education Week*, 13 November, 48.

Stewart, T. A. (1997) *Intellectual Capital: The New Wealth of Organizations*, New York: Doubleday/Currency.

Teske, P. E. and Schneider, M. (1999) "The Importance of Leadership: The Role of School Principals," a report sponsored by the PricewaterhouseCoopers Endowment for the Business of Government, Arlington, VA: The Endowment.

Thomas, A. H. (1999) "Learning from the Field: Are High Poverty, High Performing Schools Professional Learning Communities?" Unpublished dissertation, The University of Texas at Austin.

Thompson, V. A. (1961) *Modern Organization*, New York: Knopf.

United News-Journal (1991) "Leadership Characteristics and Their Definitions," Hartford, CT: United Technologies Corporation, May Special Edition, 2.

Vaill, P. B. (1984) "The Purposing of High-performing Systems," in T. J. Sergiovanni and J. E. Corbally (eds) *Leadership and Organizational Culture*, Urbana: University of Illinois Press, 85–104.

Van Manen, M. (1991) *The Tact of Teaching: The Meaning of Pedagogical Thoughtfulness*, Albany: State University of New York Press.

Weick, K. E. (1982) "Administering Education in Loosely Coupled Schools," *Phi Delta Kappan*, 63, 10: 673–6.

Wills, G. (1994) "What Makes a Good Leader?" *Atlantic Monthly*, 273, 4: 63–80.

Index

Page numbers in *italic* refer to figures and tables

ability, demonstrating 74
ability-authority, principle of 118–19
academic capital 78
accomplishment, recognizing 120
accountability 88, 118; language of 89–90;
    systems for schools 74–5; talk 121
accuracy and precision, decision- making
    100
administrative work, rational approach to
    7–8, *see also* Amoeba Theory,
    management
altruistic love 69
Amoeba Theory, management 4, 7–8;
    assumptions underlying 14–16; testing
    16–18
apprenticeship, learning as 121
Arkansas and Maine, standards 82–3
authentic: definition 90; intellectual work 91;
    learning, assessment of 92
authority: of shared ideas 29–30; sources of
    18, 54, 61, 62; why people follow leaders
    28–9
autonomy and mandates, balance 77
awareness, what is going on 131

Banner and Cannon, mutual responsibility
    73
bartering, leadership by incentives 8, 14, 34,
    50, 63–4
Barth, collegiality 108
basic: competencies 51–4; skills areas,
    standards and tests 93, 94
bees, complex adaptive systems 102–3
behavior: changing 21; leadership 20
Bennis, Warren: coordinated contributions
    38; managers and leaders 44
bonding: connections 66; leadership by 9
bridging connections 66
Bryk et al., external reviews 94
building with canvas 9–12, 16
bureaucratic authority 29
Byrne, complexity in the business world 3

California, setting science standards 85–6
capacity 110; building 47–9, 50
capital 47–8; development and school
    effectiveness 79; social and academic 78

Carey and Frohnen, community 66
causes and consequences, inner structure of
    school 6–7
central strategies and local leadership *50*
challenge of leadership 121–24; enjoying
    132–3
change: equating with leadership 41–3,
    43–5; resisting 45
changing behavior 21
character: individual 76; school 76–7, 77–8
characteristics contributing to learning 79
civic virtue 67
clients and customers, considering students
    as 73
cliques 63, 78
Cohen, March and Olsen, schools as
    organized anarchies 55
Cohen and March, tactical rules 56–7
collaborative cultures 70
collegiality 11, 66, 108
Collins and Porras, enduring companies 128
command and control leadership 128
commitment, management of 54
communication in school 130
communis and *communitas* 66, 68, 70–2
community 70–2; communities of practice
    108–9; cultural connections 63–5;
    definition of 66, 67; and diversity 66–7;
    evolution in schools 71–2; and human
    capital 48; individualism in 67–72; leader
    as builder of 50; learning community
    72–3; reasons for 62; school as 59, 61;
    successful schools 129
companies, enduring, source of stability 128
competencies for leadership 51–4
competition and comparison, student ability
    74
complex adaptive systems 101–3, *104*, 106
complexity: leadership in school
    environment 1–2; of work and mutual
    adjustment 106–9
connections: community 66–7; cultural
    63–5; shared ideas 103; valuing 130–31
conservative approach to improvement 4
constructing new knowledge 91–2
context: for leadership 1–19; in leadership
    99–100

control: of events or probabilities 104–5;
span of, organizational variable 112;
strategies 105–6, *see also* mutual
adjustment
conversation, exchange of ideas 34–5
cooperation, organization principle 117
Cuban, successful schools 97
cultural: connections 63–5; forces 103;
patterns 23
culture of school: building 27; emphasis on
6; leadership by bonding 9; role of head
96–7, 128
curriculum, academic rigor in 120–21

Darling-Hammond, learning to high
standards 127–8
Day, good leaders, definition 122
decision-making 2–3; accuracy and precision
100; centralization, degree of 116;
decision staggering 12–13; humble
12–13; influencing course of 56–7
democracy, dominance of technocracy over
45–6
democratic participation 49, 50
density of leadership, organizational
variable 112, 116
direct: leadership 110; supervision 106, 109

educational leadership 26
effectiveness: capital development and 79;
leaders 2, 21–2; link with lifeworld of
school 79–80; management of 53;
organizing for 11; and school character
78
efficiency, organizing for 10–11
effort-based schools 120
egocentric love 69
empowerment, organization principle
117–18
encouraging leadership 132
equity and uniform standards 82
Etzioni: community scrutiny and public
control 75; decision-making 3, 12–13;
'principled decentralization' 70–1
evaluations 120, *see also* tests
excellence, leadership for, eight principles
130–33
expectations, clear 120
external: audiences, creating illusion for
9–12; reviews 94, 95

fellowship in community 66, 67
Florida, school standards 82
'follow-me' leadership 28–9, 40–1, 62
form, following function 9, 78
Freedman, complex adaptive systems 101–2,
102

Fullinwider, virtues 77
future leaders, identifying and nurturing 132

gangs 63, 78
Gardner, Howard, cognitive orientation of
leadership 35
Gardner, John: beliefs and ideas 36; effective
leaders 21–2
Geertz, culture 23
goals, standards and outcomes 117
The Good High School, Lightfoot 80
Greenfield, purpose of leadership 24

Habermas, lifeworlds 77
Hargreaves and Fullan, solutions, thinking
through 101
hierarchical systems 31
High Performance Theory, management 32,
33, 34
high stakes accountability system 74
high standards: learning to 127–8; modeling
20–1
Hill and Celio, school characteristics
contributing to learning 79
human capital 47
humble decision-making 12–13
humility, leadership virtue of 123–5

ideas-based leadership 20–37, 54, 62
imagination, organizational 111, *113*
incentives 8, 14, 34; leader as motivator 50;
and mandates, strategies 46–7; rational
connections 63–4
individualism, protecting while maintaining
community 67–72
inner school structure 4–5; principles for
reaching 5–14
instructional excellence, focus on 130
intellectual: capital 48; qualities for
leadership 4–14; work, standards for 91–3
interaction, interdepartmental and
interschool 116
interpersonal climate in schools, improving
108
invert the rule, inner schools structure 5–6

Kanter, Rosabeth Moss: direct supervision
and work process standardization 109;
opportunity and capacity 109–10
knowledge-based authority 117

Lambert, leadership, definition 41
Langer, symbol and meaning 23
language of accountability 89–90
large schools 22
layered standards system 88–9, 93–5
leader, roles of 49–51, 128, 130

leaders, encouraging future 132
leadership: challenge of 121–24;
    components, heart, head and hand 39;
    definitions 41, 121–22; direct 110;
    meanings for 40; principles for 5–14, 96,
    130–33; standard prescription 3; style
    20–1, 100; substitutes for 110; theories
    30–3; views of 39–40, *see also* 'follow me'
    leadership
leadership density, organizational variable
    112, 116
leading with ideas *see* ideas-based leadership
learner, expectations placed on 120, 121
learning: as apprenticeship 121; community
    72–3; core principles contributing to
    120–21; and leadership 99–125; as
    lifelong experience 133; organizing to
    enhance 119–21; outcomes *see* standards;
    school characteristics contributing to 79;
    taking responsibility for one's own 73–4;
    teacher learning 109–10; to high
    standards 127–8
Lieberman and Miller: community 129;
    educational leadership 26; moral
    messages 26–7
lifeworld of schools 77–80, 87–8, 96–7
Lightfoot, *The Good High School* 80
Lipham, management and leadership,
    distinction between 44
local: capacity 48–9, 49; control, rebuilding
    trust 75; leadership, influence of central
    strategies *50*
localism and public disclosure 75, 95–6
love, altruistic and egocentric 69

MacBeath, Moos, Mahoney and Reeves,
    definitions of school leadership 121–22,
    123
McLaughlin and Mei-Ling Yee, opportunity
    and capacity 110
management: competencies for leadership
    51–4; and leadership, distinction between
    44; theories 30–3
mandates 46–7; and autonomy, balance
    between 77; leadership roles 49–50
March, symbolic leadership 27–8
material capital, organization-like schools
    47–8
meaning: construction of 41; for leadership
    40; management of 51–2; search for
    23
meaningfulness, principle of 118
medicine, decision-making in 12
memory, organizational 111, *113*
Midgley and Wood, competition and
    comparison 74
Mintzberg, mutual adjustment 107–8

modeling: high standards 20–1; moral
    precepts 26–7; skilled practice 121
moral: aspects, leadership 13–14, 62;
    authority 9, 29, 54; connections, cultural
    norms 34; institution, school as 33–4,
    128, 130
Morris, humility in leadership 124
Morse, bees, complex adaptive systems
    102–3
motivation 24; organizational 111, *113*;
    theory 8
mutual adjustment 106–9
mutuality, exchange of ideas 35

national standards movement 127
new leadership, roles and competencies
    38–58
Newmann et al., assessing learning 91–2
non-curriculum areas, school standards 94
normative leadership 38
norms 22, 34
North America, bias towards change 43–4

opponents, facilitating participation of 57
opportunity and capacity 109–10
organizational: intelligence 110–15; learning
    109; restructuring 6–7; theories 30–3
organized anarchies, schools as 55
organizing, principles for 117–19
outcomes, learning *see* standards
ownership and responsibility, successful
    schools 129

pedagogy 72–3
perception, organizational 111, *113*
persistence, influencing course of decisions
    56
personal: authority 28–9, 61–2; vision 39
policies and rules, implementation 11–12
policy strategies and leadership roles 49–51
post-transformational leadership 122–3
power, unequal distribution 13–14
practical intelligence 52–3
prior knowledge-base, constructing new
    knowledge 91–2
probabilities, control of 104, 105
problems, addressing 57, 131–32
procrastination 12–13
promises 64
public disclosure and localism 75, 95–6
purposing, importance of 24–8
Pyramid Theory, management 31, 33, 34

Quinn, role of leader 24

Railroad Theory, management 7–8, 15,
    31–2, 33, 34

rational: connections 63–4; and rationalistic approaches 7–8, 99–100
rationality and management theories 14–15
reading, setting standards in 86
reason, organizational 111, *113*
reasoned procrastination 12–13
recognition of accomplishment 120
reflective practice 12, 35–6
representation, setting standards 83–4
resilience, leadership for excellence 132
Resnick, organizing for learning 119–21
respect 68
responsibility: leading communities of 59–75; principle of 118; standard setting 93–4
restructuring and improvement, causes and consequences 6–7
rigor 68, 89–90
Rousseau, community 68, 69–70
rules and regulations 31, 116

Sacks, social contracts 64
Saphier and King, building cultures 27
Sarason, learning 109
Schön, which problems to solve 2
school: character, effectiveness and layered standards 76–98; as commmunity 59, 61; culture *see* culture of school; improvement 5–14, 106–9; lifeworld 77–80, 87–8, 96–7; quality review 75, 95–6; success *see* successful schools; technocratic or democratic institution 45–6
scrutiny and public disclosure, at local level 75
self-designing teams 49
self-governing teams 49
self-interest, motivation by 61–2, *see also* incentives
self-knowledge 52
self-management 49, 52–3; complex adaptive systems 102
sense and meaning, emphasis on 8–9
seven basic principles: amoeba theory 7–8; building with canvas 9–12; causes and consequences 6–7; decision-making, humble 12–13; inverting the rule 5–6; moral aspects, leadership 13–14; sense and meaning, emphasizing 8–9
shared ideas: authority of 29–30; connection by 103, *see also* ideas-based leadership
situational leadership 23
size of school, school management system 22
Skibbins, organizational intelligence 110–15
small schools 22
social: capital 49, 78; contract 63–4; educational areas, standards 93–4, 94

socializing intelligence 121
society, views of 60–1
Sowell, bias towards change 43–4
span of control, organizational variable 112
standardization of work processes or outcomes 109
standardized assessments 80–1, 91, 94
standards 32, 84–7; adopting uniform 82; differentiated 83, 87; and equity 82; for intellectual work 91–3; layered approach to 88–9, 93–5; setting 83–4, 85–6, 88–9; and standardization 32, 80–4; standards movement 80–1, 127; subjectivity of 85, 86–7; testing *see* tests
Starratt, symbolic leaders 25–6
status, exchanging for substance 56–7
Sternberg, practical intelligence 52–3
strategy: choosing 46–7; influence of central *50, see also* policy strategies and leadership roles
structure of school, inner and outer 4–5; inner structure, principles to reach 5–14; outer structure, requirements 10
students: role of 73; subcultures 63, 78
style and substance, leadership 20–1, 100
subsidiarity, principle of 84
successful schools 53, 97, 129; New York City 96–7
supervision, direct 106, 109
symbols and meaning in leadership 8, 23–4, 25–6, 27–8

teacher: development 48; isolation 108; learning 109–10
teaching standards 94
technocracy, dominance over democracy 45–6
Teske and Schneider, successful schools, New York City 96–7
tests: basic skills areas 93, 94; measuring educational progress 127; and standards 87; test scores 91
Texas, standards and standardization 81, 86, 129
time: making decisions and forwarding proposals 56; span for reaching goals, organizational variable 116
trust: management of 52; reclaiming 74–5
tutorials, organizing for efficiency 10–11

understanding the ground 131

Vaill, purposing 25
virtues 77

Weick, effective administrators 24–5
whole school quality review process 94